Take Two Psalms

...and call me in the morning

God's Prescription for Daily Wellness

Robert M. Gullberg M.D.

Table of Contents

PART TWO

King David knew God extremely well. He ascribed to God over **100 attributes** in Psalms. God will reveal insights into His character from Psalms that will give you a glimpse of His glory. Use this book as a source for individual or corporate prayer.

~Why You Should Read This Book~

"Take two Aspirins and call me in the morning" was a popular saying used by physicians well over 100 years ago. On March 6, 1899, acetylsalicylic acid (ASA), was patented by Bayer & Co. in Germany under the trade name "Aspirin". It's still one of the most highly used medications world-wide. It's active ingredient, salicin, has been used for centuries to alleviate pain and fever. Even the famous Greek physician Hippocrates (460-370 B.C.) was known to have used it. Today, about 40 billion aspirin tablets are consumed annually.

There's an alternative plan for wellness besides aspirin or other medical treatments-- *redirecting* the old standard of therapy of our problems is the theme of this book. *Take Two Psalms and call me in the morning* addresses health problems that are common in clinical practice. Some of these include:

Addiction	Anger	Boredom	Life Change
Depression	Discouragement	Fear	Guilt
Loneliness	Insecurity	Sickness	PTSD
Stress	Burnout	Worry	Moral Failure

This book is for hurting people. Essentially, it is a book of God's prescription from Psalms in response to life's struggles. The Great Physician wants to be your prime source of hope to help you cope with pain and difficulties.

Stress affects us in different ways every day. It doesn't matter what walk of life you're in... stress is there in good times and bad. For instance, your life might be rolling just fine when you get married and are pregnant with your first child, but then your baby is born 4 weeks premature with a congenital heart defect and a three-month hospitalization (not to mention that as a parent, you realize that you're suddenly responsible for the life of another human being!)…and life becomes stressful. Or your 10- year old son falls out a tree and breaks his arm…and you worry. Or maybe you're on vacation at the beach in Florida and your lounge chair collapses, crushing your index finger and requiring surgery, and you're a dentist! You will miss six weeks of work…worry sets in. Or you've been happily married for forty years when your spouse suddenly develops Alzheimer's dementia changing your relationship forever…and depression and exhaustion set in.

The list of problems that can affect our lives goes on and on and on. And these types of stresses are just the "tip of the iceberg" in terms of the hundreds of ways we can experience both mental and physical stress. But rather than medications and other therapies, the prescriptions offered here are the Psalms from the Bible. You will find that Psalms are much more precious than the effects of pills or therapy. The Psalms help redirect our mind and spirit to God who made you. God wants to care for us at all times in our lives, especially when we are struggling.

Inspired by God and primarily written by King David, Psalms is a unique book in the Bible that helps us navigate our swings of anxiety, depression, fears, guilt, and pain that occur throughout our lives. Along life's journey, we face formidable times, and psalms offers us hope, comfort, and encouragement. There is nothing we face that God can't help us overcome.

The theme of this book is that God wants us to go to Him *first,* with an honest and open heart. He is the most caring Physician in our lives. He desires to work in us through our weaknesses, which can be magnified *when we carry mental stress.* He allows us to walk through these experiences so that we can *learn* to turn our faces toward Him. It is not that doctors, counseling, friends, and medications (natural or not) can't be beneficial. It's just important that we *consider* what God has to say about our problems. Don't leave God *out of our healing equation.*

Many people may ask, "How can reading a Psalm help me more than medication for my problem?" To answer, we must understand first that most of the Psalms are *prayers to God.* The Bible teaches us that God pays as much attention to the person praying to him as the words that are read, meditated on or spoken. God wants a deep relationship with us, his adopted children. He wants to guide us and answer our prayers that we direct to him. Jesus teaches us in **John 16:24,** "Until now you have not asked for anything in my name. Ask and you will receive, and your joy will be complete." One of the most exciting things about the Christian life is the knowledge that when we pray, God is listening. Our Father is delighted when we come to him with our petitions and concerns, and the book of Psalms is rich with examples of how to pray wholeheartedly.

I am not a psychologist, professional counselor, or psychiatrist but I have been a practicing clinical physician and have cared for thousands of patients for over 30 years. Every day I see the daily mental and physical obstacles people face in their lives. Rather than pills, herbs, and therapy, I hope Going to God First will become the primary prescription for many of the battles you face. His prescription never fails.

God has answers for your problems that will change your life for the better and help to transform you, body, mind, and spirit. He may direct you to healthcare professionals, a new diet, exercise, medication, or therapy to aid you in your journey to wellness. Your journey of good health begins with him.

Psalms for Wellness is the second section of this book on pages 105-150 which will draw you closer to God. There are TWO primary parts in this section: *Learning to Go to God First* in the many circumstances in your life; and *Knowing God Better* through the Psalms. King David knew God extremely well. He ascribed to God over **100 attributes.** God will reveal insights into his character from Psalms that will give you a glimpse of his glory. Use this section of the book as a source for individual or corporate prayer.

I know you will enjoy reading this book and discover the Psalms are truly God's Prescription for Wellness. Use it for personal or group study.

Robert M. Gullberg M.D.
General Internist

THEME OF THIS BOOK:

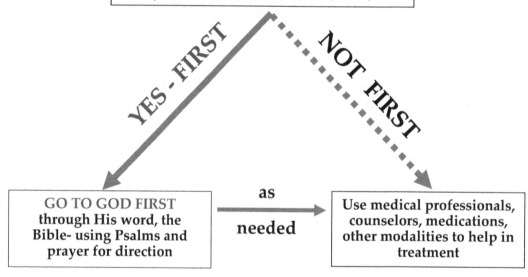

Health issues- addiction, worry (anxiety), chronic pain, fear, anger, boredom, loneliness, guilt, low self-image, discouragement, conflict, moral failure, burnout, depression' post-traumatic stress disorder (PTSD)

YES - FIRST

NOT FIRST

GO TO GOD FIRST through His word, the Bible- using Psalms and prayer for direction

as needed

Use medical professionals, counselors, medications, other modalities to help in treatment

1 | Addiction

"Addiction makes you too selfish to see the havoc you created or care about the people whose lives you have shattered."

- Anonymous

<u>Definition</u>: Addiction is defined as a repetitive habitual desire that when acted upon causes adverse and sometimes life-threatening consequences to you or those around you. The photo on the left shows a person who had a recent drug overdose of narcotics. Addiction to narcotics is epidemic in the western world today.

There are two kinds of addiction: substance (drug) addiction and behavioral addiction. <u>Substance addiction</u> is when you are addicted to a substance like alcohol (though some would argue that alcoholism is a disease), marijuana, nicotine, heroin, or cocaine. <u>Behavioral addiction</u> is a repetitive and compulsive behavior that takes over your life such as gambling, sex, food, or cell phone use.

<u>Substance addiction:</u>

- Alcohol
- Drugs- such as marijuana, stimulants, hallucinogens (LSD)
- Nicotine
- Prescription Drugs- such as opioids (Vicodin) or benzodiazepines (Valium)

Alcohol and drug abuse have plagued our culture for hundreds of years and both problems continue to thrive. The abuse of drugs starts early in life. For example, 80% of high school seniors admit to drinking alcohol.

1. *13 years of age* is the average age children experiment with drugs.
2. Alcohol is the most abused substance and the *3rd most common* cause of death in the United States.
3. 50% of all suicides and over 50% of all violent crimes are cause by people addicted to alcohol and/or drugs.
4. Over 50% of all traffic accidents involve alcohol or other drugs.
5. 80% of all domestic violence reports are somehow related to alcohol or drugs.
6. Pain killers (such as oxycodone, hydrocodone, fentanyl), tranquilizers (such as benzodiazepines like Valium) and stimulants (such as

medications for ADD-Attention Deficit Disorder) are the commonly abused prescription drugs.

7. Marijuana, cocaine, heroin, hallucinogens (LSD), nicotine, meth-amphetamine, and Ecstasy (a chemical alteration of methamphetamine) are the most commonly abused illegal drugs. All are highly addictive. If you could ask the psychiatrist Sigmund Freud about his use of cocaine, he would tell you about the power of addiction.

8. $600 *billion* is lost annually in the U.S. due to substance abuse.

9. Some scientists feel that nicotine addiction from cigarettes, cigars or "vaping" has been shown to be a stronger addiction than cocaine. Unfortunately, the effects of the tar from cigarettes have led to all kinds of cancers and lung disease such as emphysema and COPD.

<u>Put a check by an addiction(s) you have experienced (now or in the past)</u>

____Gambling
____Risky behavior
____Social media/Cell phone use
____Working yourself to the bone
____Food/carbs/sweets/wheat/caffeine
____Binge Eating
____Video Gaming
____Pornography/Sex
____Shopping
____Plastic surgery for body improvement
____Perfectionistic attitudes

Stuart Briscoe (in photo on the left), international Christian author, says this about addiction: "It is a physiological experience that results from a prior psychological experience called dependence. All of us find it relatively easy to develop a dependence on some thing or some person. Feelings of insecurity or boredom or loneliness or desire for acceptance drive us to embark on behavior that brings relief or euphoria or acceptance. As we need more and more, we move into these behavior patterns and develop a dependence. We must maintain the high because we cannot face the low. This becomes psychological dependence, which can degenerate into a physiological addiction."

Some people would argue that addiction is a disease of the brain. Others would say that addiction is a sin. Both are true. Anything that takes us away from God and separates us from him can be sin. Sin, then, is a hindrance to a right relationship with our Creator. The addict is *intent* on their addiction, and literally nothing can stop them except a powerful intervention. The addiction, often unknowingly, becomes their powerful focus in life. A relationship with God gets crowded out of their addictive lifestyle. They consciously continue to make the decision of doing their addiction, and over time feel more and more hopeless.

But addiction *also* affects neurotransmitters in the brain that bring pleasure. This is especially true of many drugs. This fact has been proven by science. That is why some say addiction is a disease. People love pleasure. Everyone pursues it. Heroin addicts feel "heroic", and thus the name, when they are addicted to this chemical so similar in structure to morphine. Fentanyl abuse has exploded. Why? Because of its powerful effects on the brain, and not just because it is a 100X more potent than morphine. Dopamine, one of the seven potent neurotransmitters in the brain, is increased with most of the substance abuse drugs. Dopamine has been shown to improve mood and euphoria. Little wonder why when people use these drugs like heroin, they can't get enough of it. Drugs give people an artificial eutopia. When without, addicts feel flat, lifeless, and depressed. Everyday life is not as pleasurable and that is why coming off the physical effects of drugs in recovery is so difficult.

Heroin addiction is disastrous. People who use heroin often require more and more to give them the same "high" because of tolerance. Soon they are on so much heroin that they can easily overdose and die. They have an increasing craving for a diminishing pleasure. Heroin may make the user feel like a "hero", but it often ends in heartache. In fact, county health departments across the U.S. are now handing out free government issued Narcan to heroin users, the anecdote of heroin excess, in case they overdose they can "self-medicate". Avoiding heroin may take God's strength only to avoid the temptation. True joy and fulfillment only come in him.

On August 11, 2014, the actor Robin Williams took his own life. The 63-year-old actor, who was loved by many fans and fellow actors, was an admitted abuser of cocaine—which he also referred to as "Peruvian marching power" and "the devil's dandruff." In 2006, he checked himself into a rehab center to be treated for an addiction to alcohol, having fallen off the wagon after some 20 years of sobriety. He later explained in an interview with ABC's Diane Sawyer that this addiction had not been "caused by anything, it's just there." Williams continued, "It waits. It lays in wait for the time when you think, 'It's fine now, I'm O.K.' Then, the next thing you know, it's not O.K. Then you realize, 'Where am I? I did not realize I was in Cleveland.'"

There is a story of a man who got on a plane and apologetically told the stewardess, "I'm going to get drunk on this flight." "I don't want to, but I always run back to the wine," he said. He got drunk, and his wife sadly cuddled him when he got off the plane, smelled his breath, and then pushed him away. He thought alcohol was a place of safety, but it was not a safe place at all. Jesus tells us to run to him so he can wrap his loving arms us and not to be ruled by fears and addictions. Jesus wants to lead us to a life of freedom.

An alcoholic that I was talking to recently has said this about the power of domination of alcohol: "The overuse of alcohol becomes an obsession of the mind, and a craving of the body. But is also a spiritual malady. It hits the mind, body, and spirit. These three aspects determine the diagnosis. Alcoholism is a disease of addiction. It's the only disease that tells the patient that they don't have it."

 Behavioral addiction such as gambling or social media may be more subtle than drug addiction, but it still robs its victims of true happiness. Look at Pete Rose (in photo on the left), the famous and prodigious baseball player on the Cincinnati Reds with over 4,200 major league baseball hits. After years of denials, he finally came clean and admitted he bet on baseball while manager of the Cincinnati Reds. Rose says he was a big-time gambler who started betting regularly on baseball in 1987 but never against the Reds, according to his autobiography, *My Prison Without Bars.* In the book, he details losing hundreds of thousands of dollars. "I didn't realize it at the time, but I was pushing toward disaster," he wrote. "A part of me was still looking for ways to recapture the high I got from winning batting titles and World Series. If I could not get the high from playing baseball, then I needed a substitute to keep from feeling depressed. I was driven, in gambling as well as in baseball. Enough was never enough. I had huge appetites, and I was always hungry." Gambling is a powerful addiction. It is estimated that in the U.S. alone about 6 million adults and about a half million teens suffer from it.

Angelina was a 15 y/o star basketball player in her high school. She excelled in her sport and was voted team captain. Her family rewarded her by purchasing her a smart phone. She loved her connection with the world around her. She slowly developed an addiction to social media and could not be without her "connection". She enjoyed seeing others comment about her basketball prowess. When she turned 16, she got her driver's license and enjoyed driving the family car to practice. She knew she wasn't supposed to text her friends and drive at the same time, but one slippery day in December, she inadvertently answered a text from her friend while driving, took her eyes off the road swerved out of her lane. She rammed into a dump truck head on and was killed instantly. How tragic to see a young life snuffed out because of a lack of not paying attention while answering a text. Could Angelina have been addicted to cell phones? Some would say "yes". Beware of this wolf dressed in sheep's clothing.

Prescription for Addiction(s): For any person with an addiction problem, God wants you to know that he can help you conquer it. He knows that because of your addiction, your focus is in the wrong place and needs to be redirected towards him. GO TO GOD FIRST.

1. Put hope in God and not in your addiction. Your addiction gives you guilt and shame. Jesus has endless compassion for you. God is stronger than your addiction.

   Psalm 65:5 You answer us with awesome deeds of righteousness, O God our Savior, the hope of all the ends of the earth and of the farthest seas

Psalm 144:2 He is my loving God and my fortress, my stronghold and my deliverer, my shield, in whom I take refuge.

2. You know how to fall into addiction. The key is to learn how to fall into the arms of your gracious God. God's grace is sufficient and made alive in your weakness.

   Psalm 67:1 May God be gracious to us and bless us and make His face shine upon us.

3. Avoid triggers. Don't build your life around your addiction, old hang outs, and friends who direct you in the wrong direction. Cry to God for help.

   Psalm 5:1-2 Give ear to my words, O Lord, consider my sighing. Listen to my cry for help, my King and my God, for to You I pray.

4. God wants to restore you and change you and make you more like Himself. You can be healed through confession to him and others. Temptation to continue in addiction is a fight though. Recovery is slow (likely years) but God desires it for you. Seek a local church body of believers who will embrace you. Join a "Celebrate Recovery" program. With services and minds centered on the Bible, Celebrate Recovery has a success rate of nearly 85%.

   Psalm 31:5 Into Your hands I commit my spirit; redeem me, O Lord, the God of truth.

5. Advice for love ones: do not shield the addict from the consequence of their actions. Do not bail them out of their misery but constantly encourage them. Seek God for guidance; consider Al-Anon.

   Psalm 48:14 For this God is our God for ever and ever; He will be our guide even to the end of our lives

Memory verse for Addiction:

   Psalm 119:114 God you are my refuge and my shield; I have put my hope in Your word.

A word on alcoholism:

As a medical doctor, I have seen the destructive force of alcoholism in a person's life numerous times. I have seen it destroy individuals and their families.

Alcoholism has been recognized for many years as a chronic and sometimes fatal *disease*. I prefer to call it *a disorder* because it has elements of disease *and* addiction. The National Council on Alcoholism and Drug Dependence offers a complete definition of alcoholism, but the simple way to describe it is "a mental obsession that causes a physical compulsion to drink." I believe *as a disease*, there are genetic, cultural, and familial predispositions that strongly impact an individual's compulsion to drink alcohol excessively and chronically.

When someone drinks alcohol, it produces a surge of dopamine in the brain's basal ganglia, an area of the brain responsible for controlling reward and the ability to learn based on rewards. With continued use of alcohol, the nerve cells in the basal ganglia "scale back" their sensitivity to dopamine, reducing alcohol's ability to produce the same "high" that it once produced. This is called a tolerance to alcohol and it causes drinkers to consume larger amounts to feel the same euphoria they once did. That is one reason alcoholics drink more and more, day by day.

Another change that chronic drinking can cause is to "train" the brain to associate the pleasure the person achieves by drinking with other "cues" in the drinker's life. The friends they drink with, the places they go to drink, the glass or container they drink from, and any rituals they may practice in connection with their drinking can all become associated with the pleasure they feel when drinking.

As *alcohol use disorder* progresses from mild to moderate to severe, the drinker experiences increasing distress whenever they are not drinking. Alcohol withdrawal symptoms can become more painful. How miserable it is to see the social, spiritual, physical, and the mental ramifications of the effects of alcoholism. There is no easy "fix" for the person struggling with alcoholism.

2 | Anger

"Anger is an acid that can do more harm to the vessel in which it is stored than to anything on which it is poured."

-Mark Twain

Definition: Anger is an emotional reaction of hostility which brings much consternation, either to somebody else or yourself. If we are honest, we will admit that anger is hard to handle at times. Having a bad temper may even make the problem worse. Let's face it, we all need help in this area. Anger is terrible for our mental and spiritual health.

America is becoming a nation of angry, short-tempered people. From road rage to airplane rage, grocery store rage and violence at youth sports events, the media has been reporting these emotional outbursts with unprecedented frequency. More than three fourths of Americans believe angry behavior has increased in places like airports and highways, according to a recent *USA Today* CNN/Gallup Poll.

Flight attendants and pilots have reported a dramatic increase in problem passengers. C. Leslie Charles, author of *Why Is Everyone So Cranky*? writes: "I'm describing a fuming, unrelenting, sense of anger, hostility, and alienation that simmers for months, even years, without relief. Eventually, all it takes is a triggering incident, usually minor, for the hostile person to go ballistic...Cell phones, pagers, and high-tech devices allow us to be interrupted anywhere, at any time. This constant accessibility, and compulsive use of technology, fragments what little time we do have, adding to our sense of urgency, emergency, and overload.

James Garbarino, human development professor at Cornell University, reports a major social shift: "There is a general breakdown of social conventions, of manners, of social controls. This gives a validation, a permission, to be aggressive. Kids used to be guided by a social convention that said, 'keep the lid on.' Today they are guided more in the direction of taking it off." Garbarino also observes an increasing "culture of vulgarity." Swear and cuss words are now common on TV and violence is promoted in much of today's youth music.

Anger affects more than just our nation. Anger affects us on the personal level in friendships and marriages. It affects people of different skin color in the conflicts over the centuries between Caucasian whites and Blacks. It affects classes in the conflicts between the bourgeois and the elite. It affects peoples of different political parties- the Democrats vs. Republicans, different countries, and different world religions. Differences of opinion can produce resentment and anger.

Put a check by the reason(s) for your anger (now or in the past):

____Getting hurt be something or someone else; why me? – mentally or physically
____Failure of yourself or others
____Political turmoil- Democratic/Republican differences
____Disappointment in a person or situation
____Frustration because of unfairness
____Lack of money
____Getting let down because of unreasonable expectations in others
____Foolish behavior of others
____Seeing innocent people suffer
____ Sin that is unforgiven
____Hypocrisy
____Other parents who do a bad job of raising their children

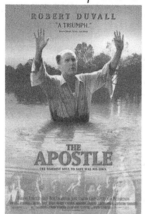

The Apostle is a movie about "Sonny" Dewey (played by actor Robert Duvall), an energetic minister leading a large ministry in Texas. When he finds out that his wife is having an affair with another minister and that they have stolen his ministry from underneath him, he *erupts in anger* and bludgeons his wife's lover to death with a baseball bat. Forced to flee town, he resumes ministry in a rural community where he tries to make sense of his life and calling as a preacher. Early in the film, facing the loss of his wife and church, Sonny goes to God in prayer. On a stormy night he paces in his room and raises his voice to heaven. His honest prayer, reminiscent of Job and some of the Psalms, conveys his anger crying out to God why he has allowed this to happen.

Police officers have it extremely tough at times. The calls that an officer fears the most are domestic disputes. When family members are fighting, it gets ugly fast—and can be dangerous. You never know what you are going to walk into when you open that door, what they might do to each other and to you. It is ugliest when husbands and wives are fighting. It is deadliest when brothers are fighting. Anger is a natural human emotion, and it is no surprise that it shows up first among members of a family.

There is a story of a soccer-loving family who helped host a boys' soccer team from Costa Rica. With their advanced ball-handling and passing skills, this elite team reached the finals of the tournament. In that final game they obviously possessed better skills than the other team, a big and physical American team that relied on bullying and cheap shots. Unfortunately, the officials were oblivious to every foul. They called nothing, allowing even outright "muggings." After the Costa Rican boys lost 2-1, one had to restrain the others from shouting at the "less than adequate" officials.

Sometimes people feel that way about God and the way God "officiates" the world. We all know that there are big problems: world hunger, a global economic crisis, mistreatment of the poor, revolutions, political oppression, and worldwide sex trafficking. Then there are also more personal problems: a friend's addiction, a marital crisis, a church split, friends who despise each other. At times we feel like crying out, "Why doesn't God intervene? Why doesn't God make a few calls and keep the game fair? Why does God let the bullies of life win?" The Psalms often allow us to bring these questions to God in our prayers. They even encourage and teach us to bring to God our disappointment and anger."

Psalm 10:1 says, "Why, O Lord, do You stand far off? Why do You hide Yourself in times of trouble?" **Psalm 13:1** says, "How long, O Lord? Will You forget me forever?" **Psalm 22:1** My God, my God, why have You forsaken me? David cries out to God to help Him in his frustration and disappointment. God wants us to go to Him in our anger and express to Him our utter disappointment.

Christian pastor and writer John Piper said this about anger: "One pastor confided in me that he gets angry easily and he often feels a lot of anger inside that his people don't recognize because of his ability to keep up a good front. I think he was speaking for a lot of us. A lot of people are angry and keep it corked inside and it ferments. Other people are different than that. They blow off as soon as anything happens to them. Others turn red in the face and grip the edge of the chair and their knuckles turn white. Others become sullen and quiet in a group and just kind of slink back out of sight. Others become very caustic and cutting with their tongue when they are angry. Whatever way you handle or respond to this rising thing called anger, it's a universal experience; and everybody has to learn to deal with it one way or the other, and most of our anger is not good."

Jesus became angry a few times as recorded in the Scriptures. However,

 his anger was perfectly justified, and righteous. What can we learn from Jesus from these situations? In **Matthew 21:12-22**, Jesus cleared the Temple of those who were buying and selling market goods there. In anger, he overturned the tables of the money changers and the benches of those selling doves. "My house shall be called a house of prayer, but you are making it a den of robbers." Note that Jesus *acted* on his anger. He did not just passively talk about it. He was mad about the *disrespect shown to his Father*.

Do you get angry about the disrespect shown to God and Jesus? He denounced the Pharisees in **Mathew 23** for their hypocrisy and put them in line. **Mark 10:13-16** is a second time that Jesus was angry when his disciples tried to keep children away from him. The disciples thought that Jesus did not have time for them. Jesus was mad about their *exclusivity*. In **Mark 16:14**, Jesus rebuked eleven of the disciples for their *lack of faith* in not believing those who had seen him after he was resurrected!

So sometimes anger is appropriate. For example, when we see all the injustice in the world that we live in. When an off-duty police officer gets killed coming to the rescue of a robbery at a local restaurant by a 15 y/o who shoots him in the chest with an automatic AK-17, it *should* get you angry. But you still need to deal with that it! If Jesus got angry, we get angry also, but not let it turn to rage. Anger is a God-made emotion. It is how we deal with anger that's important. We cannot let it get destructive. **Ephesians 4:26** says, "In your anger, do not sin. Do not let the sun go down while you are still angry, and do not give the devil a foothold."

If anger continues, it can lead to further sin. **Ephesians 4:30** says, "And do not grieve the Holy Spirit of God, ...get rid of all bitterness, rage and *anger*, brawling and slander, along with every form of malice. Be kind and compassionate to one another, forgiving each other, just as in Christ God forgave you. You can frustrate God (and His Spirit) by how you live! In **Numbers 20:8-12**, Moses was instructed by God to speak to a rock in front of his Israeli people, and then it would pour out water in a miraculous way. The people had been dehydrated in the desert and were opposing Moses' leadership. By that time, Moses was getting frustrated of the rebellious Israelites. "Listen, you rebels, must we bring you water out of this rock? Then he raised his arms and struck the rock twice with his staff. Water gushed out, and the community and their livestock drank." Because of this act of disobedience to the Lord, Moses and Aaron paid the price of the peoples' disobedience and were not permitted to bring the Israelites into the Promised Land.

The Bible teaches that anger is like a fire; it catches, destroys, and consumes. **Proverbs 27:4** states "Anger is cruel and fury overwhelming, but who can stand before jealousy?" It can sometimes be quenched by a gentle answer and patience. **Proverbs 15:1** says, "A gentle answer turns away wrath, but a harsh word stirs up anger." The New Testament gives us Jesus' example for the ideal response to provocation. It says in **2 Peter 2:21-23** that we "should follow in his steps." When they hurled their insults at him (in anger), Jesus did not retaliate; when he suffered, he made no threats. Before Jesus stood trial before Pilate, the men who guarded Jesus mocked and beat him. And they said many other insulting things to him (**Luke 22:63-65**). How did he respond? Rather than drawing on a legion of angels, he gently tolerated the diatribes in humble submission like a lamb going to slaughter. Paul reminds us in **Romans 12:19** not to take revenge but leave room for God's ability to handle the situation, either now or later.

A quick anger response to a situation may bring on additional sin. Anger can lead to other sins such as hatred, malice, murder, or gossip. When we have a fit of anger, we say things that we do not mean to say. We hurt people we do not intend on hurting. Stirring up anger produces ill-feelings and conflict. Jesus warned about the dangers of anger in the Sermon on the Mount in **Matthew 5:21-26**. In anger, we often make fools of ourselves because we do not have the "full story".

Self-control and patience are the fruits of the Spirit that represses unbridled anger. We need to let our tongues be under discipline. **1 Peter 1:13** says, "Prepare your minds for action; be *self-controlled*; set your hope fully on the grace to be given you when Jesus Christ is revealed."

Prescription for Anger: With God's help, you can deal with anger rather than have it deal with you! GO TO GOD FIRST.

1. We overcome the dangers of anger by allowing God to be our avenger. A response of anger is feeling slighted somehow and the strong desire to "get even". You begin to resent who you are angry with. Anger goes frequently with pride, wanting to do things your way. Let God help you deal with your anger. He is your faithful avenger.

Psalm 94:1 O Lord, the God who avenges, O God who avenges, shine forth.

2. Many sins we commit like anger are out in the open, but we can cover them up also. Admit you have a problem. Repent of your anger and plea with God to help you. Talk about your anger to God and that can help you "defuse" it.

   Psalm 40:12 For troubles without number surround me; my sins have overtaken me, and I cannot see. They are more than the hairs of my head, and my heart fails within me.

3. Do not let the sun go down on your anger. In other words, deal with it! Do not give the devil an opportunity in your anger. Anger leads to a multitude of other sins such as hatred, gossip, and jealousy.

   Psalm 4:4 In your anger do not sin; when you are on your beds, search your hearts and be silent.

4. Learn to ignore the little things in life that can be irritating. Major in the majors, not the minors. Learn to forgive people when they let you down, just like God forgives you. This will free you from imprisoning yourself.

   Psalm 86:5 You are forgiving and good, O Lord, abounding in love to all who call to you.

5. Keep a close check on your speech. Before you know it, your tongue with angrily get you in more trouble. God can give you the power to control your speech. This may almost seem miraculous to you.

   Psalm 77:14 You are the God who performs miracles; You display Your power among the peoples.

Memory verse for Anger:

   Psalm 103:8 The Lord is compassionate and gracious, slow to anger, abounding in love.

3   Boredom

"I'm bored with it all."

- last words of Winston Churchill,
famous Prime Minister of the United Kingdom

<u>Definition</u>: the state of being weary and restless because of a lack of interest.

Boredom is a common mental health issue that affects people of all ages. Being bored is detrimental and if not dealt with, can lead to depression. The guy on the left just retired and is looking for something to do. Sometimes life's circumstances make you suddenly bored with your time. For example, you suddenly become widowed after 50 years of marriage after your spouse dies of cancer. You have been a prime caregiver as their health slips away for months and months, happy to put your time into caring for your loved one. Death comes knocking on the door, and you are left with hours every day wondering what you can do with all the extra time on your hands.

Most people get bored at times. Almost everyone suffers from it. Surveys estimate that between 60 percent and 90 percent of Americans experience boredom at some point in their lives, as do 91 percent to 98 percent of youth. Those dog days of summer used to drag us down when we were kids sitting on the curb deciding what we could do next. As we age, time seems to go faster, but we are still challenged with monotony at times.

You may get bored doing the same thing day in and day out. You wake up every morning, go to work in a "sleepwalk" mode, come home, eat dinner, watch a sitcom on TV, and go to bed. Boredom has set in. Your weekend routine is a little different, but overall life is drudgery, and you lack a specific purpose. Boredom turns to discontent, discontent to depression.

<u>Put a check by the reason(s) for your boredom (now or in the past)</u>:

_____ Inadequate rest
_____ Inadequate nutrition
_____ Low levels of mental stimulation
_____ Lack of diversified recreational interests
_____ Loss in interest
_____ Fear of the unknown
_____ Fear of making a mistake

_____ Repetition of activity
_____ Too much time on your hands
_____ Not knowing where or how to focus your time

Here is how the best-selling author Michael Crichton described our society's need to be constantly entertained: Today, everybody expects to be entertained, and they expect to be entertained all the time… Everyone must be amused, or they will switch: switch brands, switch channels, switch parties, switch loyalties. This is the intellectual reality of Western society. In other centuries, human beings wanted to be saved from illness, or improved, freed, or educated. But now they want to be entertained. The great fear is not of disease or death, but of *boredom*.

People and especially teens tend to cling to social media and their smart phones to relieve themselves from being bored. How do Silicon Valley tech gurus design a successful app on a smart phone, an app that will hook consumers and then keep them hooked so they keep coming back to the app? Some app designers call this process "captology," or the art of capturing people's attention and making it hard for them to escape. In his book *Hooked: How to Build Habit-Forming Product*, Nir Eyal, a game designer and professor at Stanford, explains why applications like Facebook are so effective. A successful app, he writes, creates a "persistent routine" or behavioral loop. The app both triggers a need and provides the momentary solution to it. Eyal writes: Feelings of *boredom*, loneliness, or indecisiveness often instigate a slight irritation and prompt an instantaneous and often mindless action to quell the negative sensation. Gradually, these bonds cement into a habit as users turn to your smart phone app when experiencing certain internal triggers.

Even being worldly successful and having tons of money in the bank does not defeat boredom. Look at Evander "The Real Deal" Holyfield, who is a former heavyweight-boxing champion of the world. During his boxing career he earned a staggering $205 million in prize money, $92 million alone in his last five fights. Holyfield lives in a 54,000 square foot mansion in Fayetteville, Georgia. Holyfield is an avid collector of cars and has a stable of thoroughbred horses worth millions. His estate is situated on hundreds of acres, where he has built a regulation-size baseball diamond and miles of horse trails and motorcycle trails. He has also opened a restaurant in the city of Atlanta bearing his name. Though Holyfield has accomplished so much in his illustrious career and will be remembered as one of the great champions of all time, he continued to fight after losing his boxing crown. Why? In an interview with Christian author Gary Thomas, he confessed, "I continue to fight because *I'm bored*."

Monotony of the *repetitive* routine can be a fight for us in our lives as well. There is a story about a mother who walked in on her six-year-old son and finds him sobbing. "What's the matter?" she asks. "I've just figured out how to tie my shoes." "Well, honey, that's wonderful." Being a wise mother, she recognizes his victory in the Eriksonian struggle of autonomy versus doubt: "You're growing up, but why are you crying?" "Because," he says, "now I'll have to do it every day for the rest of my life."(Haha!)

There was a young couple who got married but neither one knew how to cook. One night, the wife (Hanna) decided to make macaroni and cheese—making so much that the couple could have it for two more dinners. On the fourth day, hubby next offered to cook, doubling the amount of macaroni and cheese, hoping that the huge pot would last for a week. When the couple sat down to have dinner that night, Hanna declared, "I'm sick and tired of macaroni and cheese. I can't eat any more of this."

Now imagine you had to eat the same food as the Israelites did for forty years, not a week or so! In **Exodus 16:23-26**, it says the Israelites gathered the manna each morning. They did everything they could do to make it palatable—they baked it and then boiled it. They sure did miss the delicious food that they had in Egypt (**Numbers 11:1-9**)! We may also feel that our life is not as exciting as it used to be. The food is the same and there is no variation. Through it all, we must realize that God promises to give us the nourishment we require for good health and he ultimately satisfies us. Study the following verse in Psalms.

Psalm 107:9 He satisfies the thirsty and fills the hungry with good things.

As our lifetimes advance, weeks turn into days and years turn into weeks. Chores are done and undone. Mowing the lawn is done and re-done. Shoveling the walk is done and re-done. 80,000 meals are prepared and eaten. Songs are sung and re-sung. The Bible is read and re-read. Office work is filed and re-filed. Prescriptions are called in and re-called in. The flu season comes and goes and come again next year, year after year. Life is full of events and tasks that once completed to be done again and again.

This observation is nothing new. Solomon, the wisest man who ever lived (**1 Kings 4:29-31**), wrote the book of Proverbs and Ecclesiastes. In **Ecclesiastes 1:2, 3, 9** he says, "Everything is meaningless. What does man gain from all his labor at which he toils under the sun? What has been will be again, what has been done will be done again; there is nothing new under the sun." Solomon in the end notes that our conclusive fulfillment comes from having a reverence for God and obeying his commandments (**Ecclesiastes 12:13**). We can find solace knowing that God values the ordinary mundane aspects of our lives.

 The following may give you a new way to look at being bored in the monotonous situations of life. Famous Christian theologian G.K. Chesterton (in photo on left) said this, "A child always says, "Do it again!" A grown-up does it again until they are dead. Grown-ups are not strong enough to exult in monotony. God says every morning, "Do it again" to the sun in the morning and the moon at night. It may be not automatic that every daisy is alike. It may be that God makes every daisy separately and has never gotten tired of making daisies alike. It may be that God has the eternal appetite of infancy. For we have sinned and grown older, and our Father is younger than we. Pause and see what this says about God's high view of repetition. He glories in the monotonous repetition of the universe we live in. The sun rises in the same direction every day, and when it does, God rejoices. And the sun will continue rising repetitively as a reflection of God's faithful rulership until the day he says stop! The earth, sun, moon, and stars travel repetitively in an orbit of God's choosing. He delights in this." If repetition is good enough for God, perhaps we should re-think our significant dislike of repetition.

Prescription for Boredom: God wants you to know that your boredom can be promptly treated. This is through his ability to give your life purpose during times of monotony. GO TO GOD FIRST.

1. Know that your life is meaningful and are called to a purpose. **Ephesians 2:10** says, "For we are God's workmanship, created in Christ Jesus to do good works, which God prepared in advance for us to do." Don't let free time make you feel bored. There is purpose in it. You may just need to find the purpose. God is near you always.

   Psalm 145:18 The Lord is near to all who call on Him, to all who call on him in truth.

2. Make everything you do an experience of fullness. Even if it is working on a factory line 8 hours a day. **Colossians 3:23** says "Whatever you do, work at it with all your heart, as working for the Lord, not for men." You could have the most monotonous job in life- remember God has you there for a reason. You may have to figure that out but trust him to guide you.

   Psalm 62:8 Trust in God all the time, O people; pour out your hearts to Him, for God is our refuge.

3. Make it an adventure to serve the Lord by volunteering somewhere, helping others, and praying for them. Remember that you are a representative for Christ. Look outside yourself to other. **2 Corinthians 5:20** says, "We are therefore Christ's ambassadors, as though God were making his appeal through us."

   Psalms 88:1-2 O Lord, the God who saves me day and night I cry out before you. May my prayer come before You; turn Your ear to my cry.

4. Strongly believe that God through his permissive will has you in whatever repetitive or seemingly boring situation that you find yourself. He alone can enable you to make it through. He is a God of endurance. He invented triathlons and Ironman competitions! He may choose to work in your life especially at those times. **Isaiah 40:28-31** says, "Do you not know? Have you not heard? The Lord is the everlasting God, the Creator of the ends of the earth. He will not grow tired or weary, and his understanding no one can fathom. He gives strength to the weary and increases the power of the weak. Even youths grow tired and weary (bored), and young men stumble and fall; but those who hope in the Lord will renew their strength. They will soar on wings like eagles; they will run and not grow weary- they will walk and not be faint."
   Psalm 19:1-2 The heavens declare the glory of God; the skies proclaim the work of this hands. Day after day they pour forth speech; night after night they display knowledge.

5. Develop your talents and gifts. God wants to make your life joyful and fulfilling. Allow your mind to be expanded to new passions. Many people "get stuck" in times of feeling bored. Believe me, the brain can be stretched! I recommend to my patients that they expose themselves to a new hobby every two years. It could be photography, art, music, cooking, sports, writing, volunteering, computers, teaching, sailing or some other activity. Maybe it will be a new recreational activity. God may use that time for you to re-create your passion for him. It is God who gifts us with treasures to enjoy on this earth and the next.

Psalm 145:19 God fulfills the desires of those who have awe for Him; He hears their cry and saves them.

Memory verse for Boredom:

Psalm 72:5 God will endure as long as the sun, as long as the moon, through all generations.

4 Life Change

"This is a new year. A new beginning. And things will change."

-Taylor Swift

<u>Definition</u>: To make a different position, course, or direction.

Changes in our lives are constant and we must learn how to adapt to these changes. If there is no adaptation to the changes, trouble is ahead.

One of the things that makes change difficult for us is that we are creatures of habit. For example, most of us eat the same things each day. I have a cup of hazelnut coffee every morning. That is my habit and I like doing it. We often wake up the same time every day and do not need an alarm clock. We have an internal timer in our brain that wakes us up. That's why traveling over numerous time zones can get us "out of whack" with our sleep patterns. Habits are simply engrained in us.

At 6:40 AM every day for 20 years, the king of the land had two eggs over easy with a pinch of pepper, black coffee, a glass of orange juice, and a piece of hot, buttered toast with peach jam for his breakfast. Breakfast was a important meal for him, and good nutrition got his day going in the correct direction. One day, he was served oatmeal instead of the eggs. "What? How dare the cook give me anything but my eggs this morning- I cannot live without my eggs!" in a huff, he thought. "I'm going to have that chef severely reprimanded!" Without asking the cook for a reason, he hastily criticized all the servants. "But king," the head butler exclaimed, "There has been a typhoid fever outbreak thought to be from eggs and we wanted to protect you from death!" The moral of the story: sometimes change is a good thing in our lives, even though we do not initially see why.

<u>Put a check by the reason(s) for your life change (now or in the past)</u>:

____Changing schools- grade school, middle school, high school, or college
____Changing from single to married
____A couple having children
____Moving to new geographic location
____Seasonal changes summer to winter
____Changing jobs or career
____Changing churches
____Changing or declining health
____Changing times- a tragedy or crisis
____Death of a loved one or close friend (the most common and abrupt

change that I see in my patients)
____New retirement or becoming an "empty-nester"
____Cultural or political changes

A sudden health change can have the biggest impact on our life. On December 10, 2003, *TIME* reporter Michael Weisskopf was riding with an Army convoy through the streets of Iraq's Al-Adhamiya when he noticed a small grenade had been thrown into the Humvee. He quickly took hold of the missile to throw it out of the vehicle, but it exploded before he could fully release it. He saved many lives that day, but he lost his right hand—his writing hand. What an abrupt change in his life that happened in a few seconds!

In the months that have passed since the tragic incident, Weisskopf has had plenty of time to reflect on several questions: *Why was I in Iraq, in imminent danger and so far away from loved ones? What has the whole mess taught me?* In his book *Blood Brothers*, he offers some of his conclusions. He admits to being in Iraq for "a fix." It was a unique opportunity for yet another milestone in his journalistic career, and the idea of it set his heart racing. Though he knew he should find peace in simply being a husband and a father, he wanted more. Since the incident, however, he finds such achievements pale in comparison to simply being there for those who love and need him most. He would probably argue that though he lost a hand, he gained a new perspective on life. (*Michael Weisskopf, Blood Brothers: Among the Soldiers of Ward 57 (Henry Holt and Company, 2006)*

Look at what cultural change did to a group of English boys who were evacuated to an island from Britain in Golding's book "Lord of the Flies." You likely read this book in high school English class. Its theme was the conflict between the human impulse towards savagery and the rules of civilization. Throughout the novel, the conflict is dramatized by the clash between Ralph and Jack, who represent civilization and savagery. In this book, we see how change can significantly and negatively affect people's heart attitudes. Similarly, our culture continues to change- its mores and value system, and that can be painful to many.

Solomon wrote on the vicissitudes of life and the constant changes that occur in **Ecclesiastes 3:1-8**. He said, "*There is a time for everything, and a season for every activity under heaven*":

-a time to be born and a time to die,
-a time to plant and a time to uproot,
-a time to kill and a time to heal,
-a time to tear down and a time to build,
-a time to weep and a time to laugh,
-a time to mourn and a time to dance,
-a time to scatter stones and a time to gather them,
-a time to embrace and a time to refrain,
-a time to search and a time to give up,
-a time to keep and time to throw away,
-a time to tear and a time to mend,
-a time to be silent and a time to speak,
-a time to love and a time to hate,
-a time for war and a time for peace.

Each of the above activities are 180 degrees the opposite of each other, and that describes what are lives are like sometimes—a whirlwind of change. God allows change to occur in our lives so we will look to him, our true guide and counselor who never changes.

In the study of J.I. Packer's book *Knowing God*, the immutability of God, or his unchangeableness is stressed. The setting of the Bible and especially Psalms reflects generations past—1000's of years ago. The culture was so different then. It may sometimes seem like the Bible belongs to that world, not this world. After all, don't we live in the space and computer/smart phone age? How can the record of God's Word help us now? The truth lies in God's unchangeable nature and character. He never changes. Only us and our circumstances change. As we know God better, we see that:

God is *always* merciful
God is *always* all-wise
God is *always* loving
God is *always* just
God is *always* all-powerful
God *always* shows grace
God *always* speaks absolute truth
God is *always* righteous
God is *always* omnipresent
God is *always* holy
God is *always* great and majestic
God is *always* eternal
God is *always* omnipresent
God is *always* all-knowing

And finally:

God is *always* unchangeable!

So why does our God who does not change allow us to be constantly bombarded by changing circumstances? Could it be that without change we cannot grow into the people he wants us to be? Could it be that change is a way that he uses to sculpture us? Could it be that without change we will forget about him? The answers are yes, yes, and yes!

But the facts are this: we resist change.

Reasons that we resist change:

-we lose control which can be frightful and anxiety producing
-we become fearful because of uncertainty
-everything is different and that takes getting used to
-we must develop a new reputation because no one knows us
-we may have to work harder than we did before
-with change can come ripple effects- worry and low self-esteem

-change can be painful emotionally

A 2006 medical study revealed just how difficult change is for people. Roughly 600,000 people have heart bypasses a year in America. These people are told after their bypasses that they must change their lifestyle. The heart bypass is a temporary fix. They must change their diet. They must quit smoking and drinking alcohol. They must exercise and reduce stress. The doctor is basically saying, "Change or die." You would think that a near-death experience would forever grab the attention of the patients. You would think they would vote for change. You would think the argument for change is so compelling that the patients would make the appropriate lifestyle alterations. Sadly, that is not the case. Ninety percent of the heart patients do not change. They remain the same, living the status quo. Study after study indicates that two years after heart surgery, the patients have not altered their behavior. Instead of making changes for life, they choose death. Change is that difficult. Most heart patients choose not to change. They act as if they would rather die. *Thom S. Rainer and Eric Geiger, Simple Church (B & H Publishing Group, 2006), p. 229.*

Change in our lives can bring uneasiness, nervousness, anger, and sometimes depression. That is why by nature we often like our "comfort zones" and to minimize change. For example, we like our traditions, whether it be personal or family. Traditions can often bring on warm fuzzies for us. Traditions are about non-change. We have traditions for birthday parties, turkey dinners at Thanksgiving, Easter egg hunts at Easter, fireworks and cookouts on 4th of July celebrations, time off work on Labor Day, Memorial Day picnics, summer vacations with family, and Santa Claus at Christmas, the celebrated time of Jesus Christ's birth. But there is a warning about certain traditions…they can lose their freshness.

South American evangelist Luis Palau (in photo on left) tells a story

 about a misplaced tradition. A wealthy European family decided to have their newborn baby baptized in their enormous mansion. Dozens of guests were invited to the elaborate affair, and they all arrived dressed to the nines. After depositing their elegant wraps on a bed in an upstairs room, the guests were entertained royally. Soon the time came for the main purpose of their gathering: the infant's baptismal ceremony. But where was the baby? No one seemed to know. The child's governess ran upstairs and returned with a desperate look on her face. Everyone searched frantically for the baby. Then someone recalled having seen him asleep on one of the beds. The baby was on a bed all right--buried beneath a pile of coats, jackets, and furs. The object of that day's celebration had been forgotten, neglected, and nearly smothered.

Similarly, the birth of Jesus that we celebrate at Christmas can easily be hidden beneath the piles of *traditions* and cultural observances of the season. We need to enter every Advent season asking, "Where's the baby?" Be careful that your own Christmas traditions do not smother the real Jesus who is the true Reason of the season.

<u>Prescription for Life Change</u>: God wants you to know that any change can be dealt with effectively if you put God in the driver's seat. Learn to GO TO GOD FIRST, the author of peace and control.

1. God's presence in your life will help you handle change. He is your true and absolute guide.

   Psalm 48:14 For this God is our God for ever and ever; He will be our guide even to the end.

2. God is our solid foundation in the middle of change. In **Matthew 7:24-29**, Jesus teaches us to be faithful and obedient to him, the Rock, to weather the storms of life. Your circumstances may change, but they do not change the validity of God's love for you.

   Psalms 31:2-3 Turn Your ear to me, come quickly to my rescue; be my rock of refuge, a strong fortress to save me. Since You are my rock and my fortress, for the sake of Your name lead and guide me.

3. God *never* changes and that is a huge help to steady you. *He wants to communicate with you* in the middle of change that you experience. The writer of **Hebrews in 11:12** tells us that Jesus is our only true security in a wavering world.

   Psalm 88:9b I call to you, O Lord, every day; I spread out my hands to You.

4. God's words in the Bible are true and do not change. That is a primary safeguard for you.

   Psalm 119:89, 160 Your word, O Lord, is eternal; it stands firm in the heavens. All Your words are true; all Your righteous laws are eternal.

5. Remember although there can be difficulties with change, it is part of life. You must learn how to prepare for it. God may allow a purposeful and directional life change for you. He is in control, not you. Give him the burden of your feelings.

   Psalm 73:28 But as for me, it is good to be near God. I have made the Sovereign Lord my refuge; I will tell of all Your deeds.

<u>Memory verse for Life Changes:</u>

Psalm 85:8 I will listen to what God the Lord will say; He promises peace to His people.

5 | Depression

"I was not happy, especially when I had a second surgery on my foot, I was definitely depressed. I cried all the time. I was miserable to be around."

- Serena Williams,
Tennis champion

<u>Definition</u>: a mental disorder marked by sadness, apathy, inactivity, and self-depreciation with a lowering of vitality or functional ability.

The National Institute of Mental Health (NIMH) estimates that 16.2 million U.S. adults had at least one major depressive episode in 2016. The World Health Organization (WHO) named depression the second most common cause of disability worldwide after cardiovascular disease, and it is expected to become number one in the next ten years. In the United States, 5 to 10 percent of adults currently experience the symptoms of major depression, and up to 25 percent meet the diagnostic criteria of depression during their lifetime, making it one of the most common conditions treated by primary care physicians. At any given time, around 15 percent of American adults are taking antidepressant medications.

<u>Put a check by the reason(s) for your depression (now or in the past)</u>:

_____ Aging with infirmities of body and mind
_____ A change in health condition- cancer, heart disease, stroke, chronic pain, thyroid disease, consequence of diabetes- such as blindness, neuropathy
_____ Trauma- such as spinal cord injury after a motor vehicle accident or fall
_____ Grief or loss of a loved one- person or pet
_____ Medication side effects
_____ Sin that is unforgiven, or an unrepentant attitude
_____ Genetics- perhaps a mother or grandfather had depression
_____ Drugs- such as alcohol (causes nervous system depression) disorder and others
_____ Stressful events in life- retirement, empty-nesting, significant change in one's life, moving to a new environment

_____ Fear of the future- young or old
_____ Relationship breakdown with hurtful emotions
_____ Financial hardship
_____ Loneliness (isolation) or boredom- discussed in other chapters
_____ PTSD- post traumatic stress disorder- discussed in a different chapter
_____ Seasonal changes- the "wintertime" blues, or S.A.D.- Seasonal Affective
Disorder, when people struggle with less natural light
_____ Excessive smartphone use

Depression is *so* common in our medical practice. In many cases, there isn't one singled-out cause for an individual's depression. Instead, it results from a mixture of things: genetics, past negative memories, current circumstances, and more. Most commonly, we see a *reactive* depression. There is an event in the life of the individual which is painful (physical, mental, or spiritual), and the reaction to that event is depression. Just like Serena William's depression from her foot surgeries, when people get out of their normal routine, they can become more depressed, especially when there is pain involved.

Recently a 53 y/o patient fell 18 feet off a ladder while cleaning out

gutters at his home. He hit the ground so hard that he shattered his pelvis, hip, shoulder, and ankle. He had internal injuries to the spleen. In the manner of seconds, not only were his bones shattered but also his life. To recover, it will take six months of rehabilitation. He will be dependent on others to take care of him after numerous surgeries. He will have pain like he has never experienced. He will likely need narcotics for pain control and will deal with their potential side effects. He will be away from his home for a time. He will need to learn how to walk again. All because of a three second fall off a ladder, this individual will face reactive depression square in the face for many months! How accidents like this can change our lives in the twinkling of an eye.

P.R. is a healthy 82 y/o female battling ongoing grief and depression from the death of her husband after 61 years of marriage. He died of a fast-growing cancer three years ago and she helped take care of him while he was in hospice. Now that he is gone, she claims, "I cannot get him out of my mind, I miss him so much. I feel paralyzed. I just don't know what to do!" "I don't know why God still wants me around here. My husband and I had such a wonderful life together. I felt like half of my body was cut off." She has developed insomnia and chronic daytime fatigue because of her reactive depression.

Another patient was recently involved in a tragic car accident. He was driving in his van on a highway out to a job site, and a young woman turned left into his vehicle head on, smashing his front end and severely injuring him. She was on her cellphone texting and stated that she did not even see his vehicle! The impact and whiplash were so great that his spinal cord was severed. Paralyzed from the waist down, he was transferred to a tertiary medical center, where he died two weeks later of complications of internal injuries and aspiration pneumonia. Even if he lived, the rest of his life would have been in a wheelchair. The depression invoked on his middle-aged wife, brother, mother, and father is profound; the harsh reality of his early death is one that they will deal with the rest of their lives. Just because of a few seconds of texting while driving. What a tragedy.

Patient Health Questionnaire - 9

Over the last two weeks, how often have you been bothered by any of the following problems?	Not at all	Several days	More than half the days	Nearly every day
Little interest or pleasure in doing things	0	1	2	3
Feeling down, depressed, or hopeless	0	1	2	3
Trouble falling or staying asleep, or sleeping too much	0	1	2	3
Feeling tired or having little energy	0	1	2	3
Poor appetite or over eating	0	1	2	3
Feeling bad about yourself - or that you are a failure or have let yourself or your family down	0	1	2	3
Trouble concentrating on things, such as reading the newspaper or watching television	0	1	2	3

Depression is often a complex problem that can be long term or short-term depending on the stressor. In men, depression can manifest as anger. In women, depression will frequently manifest as sadness and crying. One way to "quantify" depression in our office to use the PHQ-9 (Patient Health Questionnaire - 9) or the Beck Depression Inventory. What are nine bothersome problems that people experience when depressed? These include: 1) little interest or pleasure in doing things 2) feeling down and hopeless 3) trouble falling asleep, staying asleep, or sleeping too much 4) feeling tired or having little energy 5) poor appetite or overeating 6) feeling bad about oneself- or that you are a failure or have let yourself or your family down 7) trouble concentrating on things, such as reading the newspaper or watching television 8) moving or speaking so slowly that other people have noticed, being so fidgety or restless that you have been moving around a lot more than usual, and 9) having thoughts that you would be better off dead or of hurting yourself in some way. By evaluating a point system based on these questions, we can get a better handle on a person's depression- is it minimal, mild, moderate, moderately severe, or severe. Then we can assess the need for more specific future therapy.

Depression can have a very dark side and cause ruthless mental torment. It can escalate to suicide when an individual sees no hope for tomorrow. Look at these celebrity examples who have taken their own lives likely in a fit of depression:

-Anthony Bourdain, age 61. He was a chef and best known for his show "No Reservations," who died from suicide on June 8, 2018.
-Kate Spade, age 55. She was an iconic fashion designer and mother who died by hanging herself in her Manhattan, New York, apartment on June 5, 2018.
-Chester Bennington, age 41. He was the lead singer of Linkin Park and hung himself July 20, 2017.

-Chris Cornell, age 52. He was the lead singer of Soundgarden band who died by hanging in 2017.

-Aaron Hernandez, age 27. He was a former New England Patriot and NFL star who died by hanging in his jail cell in 2017.

-Robin Williams, age 63. He was a famous comedian who likely committed suicide in 2014 (he likely had early Lewy body disease, a form of dementia). Williams, like comedians John Belushi and Chris Farley who died previously of drug-related deaths, lived with long-term depression and addiction.

The number of suicides that happen daily rarely make national news. But when a celebrity commits suicide, it's instant news. It hits the headlines because, in one sense, on the outside it does not always make sense. Riches, success, and fame certainly do not always add up to suicide. But depression is undoubtedly the fast lane on the highway that so often leads to the place of self-destruction. - *from Ray Comfort, The Final Curtain, pgs. 7-8*

In our culture, by now, we have learned that materialism cannot satisfy us. Or have we? Materialism is the pursuit of accumulated wealth of *things*. Think about anything that you have purchased which is new. A new car, bike, stereo, watch or even a new house. The world offers us happiness through material possessions: a new smartphone, a new watch, or new clothes. The problem is this: yesterday, we were happier with our possession than today. Just how long does it take newness to wear off? Not long. God created us to enjoy his riches and nothing else will satisfy. There are no replacements. Everything else gets old. Deep down we are spiritual beings and cannot get fulfillment with material goods alone. Material things and money do not prevent depression or suicide.

Depression is affecting young people in our country at a record pace.

Why? Possibly the smartphone. In Jean M. Twenge's article, "Have Smartphones Destroyed a Generation," (*The Atlantic* (9-17)), she writes this: "More comfortable online than out partying, post-Millennials are safer, physically, than adolescents have ever been. But they are on the brink of a mental-health crisis. The number of teens who get together with their friends nearly every day has dropped by more than 40 percent from 2000 to 2015; the decline has been especially steep recently. It is not only a matter of fewer kids partying; fewer kids are spending time simply hanging out. The roller rink, the basketball court, the town pool—they've all been replaced by virtual spaces accessed through apps and the web. A recent survey asked teens how happy they are and also how much of their leisure time they spend on various activities, including non-screen activities such as in-person social interaction and exercise, and screen activities such as using social media, texting, and browsing the web. Those who spend six to nine hours a week on social media are 47 percent more likely to say they are unhappy or depressed.

Those who spend an above-average amount of time with their friends in person are 20 percent less likely to say they're unhappy."

Scratches and scrapes are for band aids, but depression is not. There are no "easy fixes". Sometimes that last thing we want to hear is a verse from the Bible or an encouraging word from a friend when we are hurting, especially if "they have not walked in your shoes".

Answers are frequently not easy when we feel like we have a dark cloud over us, but it is wise to use resources available to us and check out some key Psalms when life seems hopeless. God desires above all else to be your source of victory over life's difficulties. The writer of Psalms knew a lot about depression, and most assuredly, his words will help you get out of the rut that you are in. King David made some bad decisions at times. He sinned plenty and always repented- God loved him dearly for this. His grief was a burden and his soul weary. (see Psalms 6 and 13). These Psalms will come alive and touch you deeply.

Prescription for Depression: God wants you to know that he can help you, comfort you, and give you inner joy in your times of depression. He can deliver you "out of the pit of despair" and give you hope forever. Learn to GO TO GOD FIRST; he is the best anti-depressant that there is! He may lead you to more therapy after you have turned to him for guidance.

1. Grieving for the loss of a loved one can pull you towards depression. It forces you to acknowledge that there is aching pain in your heart. Coming face to face with a difficulty causes deep anguish. Your hope is in God's ability to hear your cries and uplift you out of what seems to be chaos. One must fight the 'cousins' of loneliness and boredom that can come with the loss of a loved one.

   Psalms 6:6-9 I am worn out from groaning; all night long I flood my bed with weeping and drench my couch with tears. My eyes grow weak with sorrow; they fail because of all my foes. The Lord has heard my cry for mercy; the Lord accepts my prayer.

2. Above all, the depressed individual lacks mental comfort. Only God can give you ultimate comfort. Everything else is secondary.

   Psalm 23:4 Even though I walk through the valley of the shadow of death, I will fear no evil, for you are with me; your rod and your staff, they comfort me.

   Psalm 71:20-21 Though you have made me see troubles, many and bitter, You will restore my life again; from the depths of the earth You will again bring me up. You will increase my honor and comfort me once again.

3. God longs for you to go to Him so that He can instill hope and encouragement in you.

Psalm 146:5-6 Blessed is the person whose help is God and whose hope is in the Lord their God, the Maker of heaven and earth, the sea, and everything in them—The Lord, who remains faithful forever.

4. The question *Why?* is always a tough one in times of depression. Sometimes the answer is obvious, and sometimes it is not. God wants you to look toward him despite questions and find joy for the future.

    Psalm 43:5 Why are you downcast, O my soul? Why so disturbed within me? Put your hope in God, for I will yet praise Him, my Saviour and my God.

    Psalm 16:11 You God, have made known to me the path of life; You will fill me with joy in Your presence, with eternal pleasures at Your right hand.

5. Fear of the unknown can be depressing. What will happen in the future? Will the chemotherapy work for my cancer? Will I get the new job? How long do I have to wait? What if my headache pain does not get better? What if my husband does not come home from his overseas deployment in the army? God yearns for you to give him all your fears.

    Psalm 27:1 The Lord is my light and my salvation—whom will I fear? The Lord is the stronghold of my life—of whom shall I be afraid?

Memory verse Depression:

Psalms 25:16-18 Turn to me and be gracious to me, for I am lonely and afflicted. The troubles of my heart have multiplied; free me from my anguish. Look upon my affliction and my distress and take away all my sins.

6 | Discouragement

"The Christian life is not a constant high. I have my moments of deep discouragement. I have to go to God with tears in my eyes, and say, 'O God, forgive me,' or 'Help me'."

-Billy Graham

<u>Definition</u>: a loss of confidence or enthusiasm; dispiritedness. The discouraged person has "lost heart" or lost courage to endure.

Discouragement is the act of being discouraged, and virtually every person is affected by it one time or the other. At times, we can be exposed to discouraging problems daily. When discouragement crescendos in severity, it will lead to defeat and then depression (discussed in Chapter 5). The things in a person's life that cause depression certainly cause discouragement, but not necessarily the other way around. If the great man of faith Billy Graham dealt with discouragement, so will we. No one is safe from this problem, and there is nothing that the Devil wants more for you than to get you so dejected that you cannot function normally. It is important to differentiate disappointment from discouragement. Disappointment is when your plans are disrupted. You have planned a high school outdoor graduation party for your daughter and the afternoon of the party, a torrential thunderstorm occurs causing you to cancel your plans. That breeds disappointment, not discouragement. Discouragement is more far-reaching than disappointment. Someone who is discouraged has lost their will, their desire to fight, and "lack courage" to go on. A family who moves to the west coast of Florida only to have a hurricane flatten and destroy their home brings on a wave of not only disappointment but more so discouragement.

<u>Put a check by the reason(s) for your discouragement (now or in the past):</u>

_____When other people let you down because of high expectations on them
_____When you let yourself down because of sin or moral failure
_____When you get filled with doubt
_____When you are so inwardly focused, you are no worldly good
_____When you do not perform as well as you would like to
_____When you are rejected by another person or group
_____When you are criticized by others

_____When you are tired and worn out
_____When you lose control of your life
_____When you are focused on the world's view of things, not God's
_____When you lose confidence in your purpose
_____When you see your loved ones' health decline
_____When you experience tragedy of any kind

Some illustrations of discouragement seen in my patients in the last month:

- a Mom and Dad are discouraged because their adult son must live with them because of a heroin addiction and has lost his job.
- a young mother of three is recently divorced and does not have enough money to pay her bills.
- an elderly lady is discouraged because her husband of 60 years is developing Alzheimer's disease
- a young father of two daughters is discouraged because his wife was recently diagnosed with a brain tumor
- a teenager who is the captain of his soccer team is discouraged because of a severe knee injury that will keep him out of competitive soccer for a year
- a middle-aged woman is discouraged because she just found a breast lump and breast cancer runs in her family
- a middle-aged woman had an elective knee replacement and a year later found out the prosthesis is loose.

My life's work revolves around caring for sick patients in the hospital.

These dear patients are sometimes in a lot of pain because of severe organ dysfunction (heart, lung, kidney, liver) or infection. Perhaps they have a brain abscess, a serious bone infection, vertebral fracture, peritonitis, a massive stroke, or a heart valve infection. Some may be so sick they live in nearby nursing homes because of their infirmity. They are unable to live at home. Hospitals and skilled facilities are nice when you need them, but they are not like the sweetness of home. The normal meals and foods that one likes are not available, and often there is a dependence on a nurse or nursing assistant to get to the bathroom. The patient questions how long it will take to get well again. The patient can feel like a prisoner in the hospital. The normal routine of life is brought to a standstill and that is discouraging!

No one is immune to discouragement, but how we respond to these difficult times might define us. If you do not have an ability to persist despite hardship, then discouragement is most likely going to haunt you.

There is a story of a cartoonist named Tom Toro which teaches us how to defeat discouragement: persistence. He knew what discouragement was after over 600 rejections. Most of us would have given up! Up to his neck in debt, directionless, feeling lost, Tom Toro moved back into his parents' place and slipped into a dark depression because of discouragement. But things started to change when Toro went to a used book sale in his hometown. He opened a cardboard box and found an old stack of _The New Yorker_ magazines. He said,

"For some reason, I was drawn toward and started riffling through them. Something just clicked. And I started drawing again." Toro decided to submit some of his cartoons to the magazine. Shortly after that, he received a reply. It was his first rejection note, of the many still to come. Toro said, "*The New Yorker* found the way to most courteously and most briefly reject people. It's just beautiful. You feel so honored to receive it and yet it's a brushoff."

A year and a half later, Toro had a pile of rejection letters. This continued until Bob Mankoff, the cartoon editor at *The New Yorker*, gave Toro some honest and specific feedback. Mankoff said he did not see any joy in Toro's cartoons. Toro threw everything that he had done previously out the door, sat down with a blank sheet of paper. Recalling Mankoff's advice, he tried to draw from the heart. He was still receiving rejection letters in the mail, but his cartoons were getting better. Toro was finding his style. And then, one day, he wandered into his office to check his email. He said, "I went in there, logged in, and there sitting at the top of my inbox was an email. The subject line read, 'Cartoon Sold.'" It was the 610th drawing Toro had submitted to The New Yorker.- *"How'd a Cartoonist Sell His First Drawing? It Only Took 610 Tries," NPR (1-25-15).*

A problem with discouragement is that it causes us to look inward at our own shortcomings and frailties. We begin to lose hope. This can be so hard on us that we lose our *will* to continue. This is one of Satan's main weapons in the fight to win over your allegiance. He wants to make us discouraged so that our faith towards God wanes and our doubts about God increases. He *wants* us to focus on our shortcomings. Then we will be no earthly good to anybody else.

When the apostle Peter got out of the fishing boat and walked on water in the Sea of Galilee, it was only when he looked at the strong wind and took his eyes off Jesus that he started sinking (**Matthew 14:22-33**). His problem was having the wrong focus. He shifted from Jesus to the rough waves that he was facing. That is what happens to us. So often we have a "pity party" for ourselves when we lose control. We look inward and become self-absorbing. We think God is not working. But he is! God has not lost control.

<u>Prescription for Discouragement</u>: God wants you to

know that he can come to the rescue with any discouragement that you are enduring. He can energize your heart. He can give you the drive to continue. Learn to GO TO GOD FIRST.

1. Discouragement can often be from not knowing how God is working in your life. Learn to trust Him completely. He is in control. He knows what He is doing! Sometimes He allows difficulties so that you can learn to look to Him for help. Put God ahead of your problems.

    Psalm 20:7 Some trust in chariots and some in horses, but we trust in the name of the Lord our God.

2. Call on God to help you persevere. He is the God of persistence.

Psalm 111:3 Glorious and majestic are His deeds, and His righteousness endures forever.

3. Keep well rested in your battle. Good nutrition and good rest are a must. Pray to the Lord for good strength and rest in Him.

    Psalm 91:1 He who dwells in the shelter of the Most High will rest in the shadow of the Almighty.

4. God can remove your faintness of heart and give you strength to keep on keepin' on.

    Psalm 46:1 God is our refuge and strength, an ever-present help in trouble.

5. Find encouragement in God's promises and His power when you are downhearted. Know that Satan is at work trying to derail you and keep you in a funk. Be strong in God and look outward from yourself. Stay proactive and intentional in your faith.

    Psalm 89:13 God's arm is endued with power; His hand is strong, His right hand exalted.

Memory verse for Discouragement:

Psalm 86:2 Guard my life, for I am devoted to you. You are my God; save your servant who trusts in You.

7 | Fear

"The presence of fear does not mean you have no faith. Fear visits everyone. But make your fear a visitor and not a resident."
— author Max Lucado

<u>Definition</u>: an unpleasant emotion caused by the belief that someone or something is dangerous, likely to cause pain, or a threat.

Dorothy Gale of Kansas, the Scarecrow, Tinman, and cowardly Lion were all exceedingly fearful of the wicked witch (played by actress Margaret Hamilton in photo on left) in the classic film "The Wizard of Oz." They were not the only ones! I remember watching the film while growing up and being so afraid of the witch that I would have to close my eyes when she appeared. The more I watched the Wizard of Oz over the years, the less afraid I became. I realized that my fear of her was "all in my head". But I must admit, she gave my siblings and I nightmares for years early on! At that time in my life, that fear was very real.

Fear is common to all of us and can knock on our door at any age.

<u>Put a check by the reason(s) for your fear (now or in the past)</u>:

_____ Fear of dying- thanatophobia
_____ Fear of mixing with people- social phobia
_____ Fear of heights- 5% of the world's population- acrophobia
_____ Fear of closed spaces- claustrophobia
_____ Fear of open spaces- agoraphobia
_____ Fear of speaking in public- glossophobia
_____ Fear of insects- entomophobia
_____ Fear of snakes- ophidiophobia
_____ Fear of flying- pteromerhanophobia
_____ Fear of the dark
_____ Fear of violent weather- astraphobia
_____ Fear of germs
_____ Fear of dogs- cynophobia
_____ Fear of going to the doctor or dentist
_____ Fear of needles- trypanophobia
_____ Fear of failure
_____ Fear of drowning- aquaphobia

_____ Fear of strangers- xenophobia

Many fears are natural for us, such as when you are prescribed a new medication by your healthcare provider and you wake up the next day with swollen lips and you cannot breathe! Having a bad reaction like this may paralyze your thinking into the future so you do not want to take any new medications.

Fear that we experience comes from within or without. It can come on suddenly, without a notice. I see the problem of fear on a regular basis in my patients. Fear can produce an avalanche of other emotions- anxiety or worry, panic, or depression to name a few. If fear affects your ability to function in day to day life, you might have one of the phobias listed on the first page of this chapter.

We never ask for an illness in our lives so we can "learn from the experience". It just lands upon us like an invasive Japanese beetle on a rose bush. It comes and zaps you of your energy. You wake up one day healthy and all the sudden you feel an enlarged lymph node in your neck. It is bigger than it should be you think. You go to your doctor and a biopsy is ordered. Your fear of the unknown and future escalates. *Is it cancer*? If it is, what kind of treatment will I need? You are suddenly incapacitated mentally. You go to work and just go through the motions. All you can think about is your problem that it might be cancer. The biopsy is lined up for the next week. Why do I have to wait so long? You fear the worst. You are afraid of what might happen to you and how it will affect your family. What will happen to your loved ones if I do not make it? You finally go through the biopsy and wait the dreaded 24 hours for the results from the pathologist. Your internist calls you the next day and you breathe a sigh of much needed relief. "It's benign," he tells you, "And it's just a cyst." Just as suddenly, life is back to normal. Thank goodness. What an agonizing two weeks of fear!

The fear of death is one of the most common phobias. Actor and comedian Woody Allen famously quipped, "I'm not afraid of death; I just don't want to be there when it happens."

In his book, *The Final Curtain*, Ray Comfort writes about American actress Amanda Peet (born 1972) who has appeared in film, stage, and television. She appeared on "The Late Show" with Stephen Colbert and put him into a very awkward moment. Things got real when Colbert asked Peet about her HBO show *Togetherness*. On the show, many of the characters struggle through midlife crises:

> Stephen Colbert: "You've got a lovely life. What do you know about a mid-life crisis, is this a stretch for you?"
> Amanda Peet: *"No!* Forty-four is ... quite something."
> SC: "You don't look like a personal crisis to me. What is your crisis?"
> AP: "I fear death!"
> SC: "Okay. ... Well ... Keep it light. We all die. It's the late-night talk show, keep it light, keep it light. Maybe you'll go to heaven. You'll die and go the heaven."
> AP: "Okay. That's where I need help. You're Catholic, right? I'm Jewish."
> SC: "What do you believe?"
> AP: "I need to know what to believe in!"

SC: "Like, what happens when you die?"
AP: "Yes. I don't want to be a bag of dust!"
SC: "I don't really know ... I don't know what happens. I kind of believe, I kind of want the pearly gates and all that.
AP: "That is not inspirational."
SC: "Not helping?"

How do others deal with their fear of death? Most do not talk about it. But the wisest man in the world did. His name was Solomon. He said this in Ecclesiastes 7:2: "It is better to go to a funeral than to go to a house of feasting, for death is the destiny of every person." Adversity in life reminds us that life is short. Most agree that we learn more about God from the tough times than from the happy times.

The New York Times in 2015 reported that veteran television commentator Larry King "was obsessed with death." His day began with reading through obituaries, and he wonders "who will give the eulogy at his funeral." He thinks it might be Bill Clinton, and then his face becomes blank. "But I won't be there to see it." King has had "a heart attack, quintuple bypass, prostate cancer, diabetes, and seven divorces." He was 77 years old when the television news station CNN dropped him and increased his awareness that there will come a day when he dies. When he learned from television of the death of Osama bin Laden, this drove him to jump up on his feet. "I needed to be on the air. I needed a red light to go on." He realized he "had nowhere to go." To deal with his anxiety about aging and death, he takes human growth hormone pills, four of them each day. He intends on his body to be frozen (the use of liquid nitrogen) so that someday he will live again (Walt Disney has reportedly done the same thing). *The New York Times* writer reports: "It's nuts, concedes King— but at least it gives him a shred of hope." Larry King says, "Other people have no hope." --*King's morbid fixation, The Week, (9-11-15)*

There is no true hope without God.

We can categorize fear into two major reaction types. The first is the fear that comes from an *outside* influence that you can control. This is common and sometimes easy to manage and sometimes not. The iconic NFL football coach and television commentator John Madden (in photo on left) absolutely hated to fly but it was necessary for him to travel quite a bit around the country from New York to Los Angeles commentating on NFL football games. To deal with his fear of flying, he stayed on the ground by driving from city to city in a large bus! This was well known by TV networks and publicized. To put it simply, he practiced *avoidance* to conquer his fear.

If your fear is closed spaces, do not go into an elevator or get an MRI.
If your fear is heights, then do not get close to a ledge.

If your fear is speaking in public, then don't be a public speaker.
If your fear is the dark, then keep the lights on.
If your fear is dogs, then don't own one and stay away from them.
If your fear is tornadoes and hurricanes, then avoid them by living in a part of the country where these storms don't occur.
If your fear is the doctor or dentist, then you stay away from going to their office but you will likely suffer for it later.

The answer to these kinds of fear is straightforward- avoidance.

A second category of fear is related to the unknown that you have little control over. This kind of fear tends to be *inward* related to your mind conjuring up a trembling timidity:

- It is 2AM in the morning and you think you hear a burglar in your house. Suddenly you have the 'flight or fight hormone' (adrenaline) response causing your heart rate to go up, you feel the tension, you sweat profusely, and begin to hyperventilate. You are fearful of what might happen. You run downstairs a spot a chipmunk in your kitchen! At least it is not a burglar!
- you get a call from a state trooper who reports to you that your daughter was involved in a serious car accident. Your child is alive but may possibly has a whiplash injury. You are fearful of what might happen to your daughter.
- a bad storm whips through your area and a category 5 tornado is sighted 10 miles from your house headed your way. The electric power is off, and you hunker down in the basement with your kids. You are fearful of what might happen to you, your family, and your house.

In 1957, Melba Pattillo Beals was selected as one of the first of nine African American students to integrate in the all-white Central High School in Little Rock, Arkansas. In her book, "I Will Not Fear: My Story of a Lifetime of building Faith under Fire, she gives an eyewitness account of the discrimination she had to face every day as a young teenage student. How did she deal with her fears? She quoted Bible verses to herself to bolster her faith. She focused on God's presence with her, and this gave her the tenacity to remain firm in her faith.

Although times and situations change, we must all endure obstacles in life that may bring on fear. These circumstances can cause us to give in to apprehension. Through the Bible, we learn that whatever troubles overtake us, Jesus is with us. It is during those times that we can get encouraged that our God is Emmanuel, or "God with Us". Many of us have had some trouble in our past causing negative memories. Some of us are incapacitated going into the future because of fear of the unknown. We must learn to live in the present. Helen Mallicoat has penned a poignant poem that exemplifies this *fact*:

I was regretting the past and fearing the future.
Suddenly my Lord was speaking: "My name is I Am."
He paused. I waited. He continued.
"When you live in the past, with its mistakes and regrets,
it is hard. I am not there. My name is not I was.

When you live in the future, with its problems and fears,
It is hard. I am not there. My name is not <u>I will be</u>.
When you live in the moment, it is not hard. I AM here.
My name is <u>I AM</u>."

The Bible refers to the word "fear" about 500 times! Why would God write so much about this subject? Simple. He knew that we would need to be influenced *away from* fear. He meets the subject head on. Here are seven examples-

-Abraham, the great Jewish patriarch, became fearful in his many war battles. God told him in **Genesis 15:1, "**Don't be fearful Abraham, for I will defend you."
-Joshua fought fear of his enemies during war. In **Joshua 8:1**, the Lord encourages Joshua not to be frightened and discouraged.
-King David was recurrently afraid. He wrote **Psalm 34** in response to his fear. He was being stalked by King Saul and feared for his life.
-Isaiah fought fearfulness as he told the Israelites to repent. God told him in **Isaiah 41:10** "Do not fear, for I am with you; do not be dismayed, for I am your God. I will strengthen you and help you; I will uphold you with my righteous right hand."
-Jonah was afraid for his life! **Jonah 1:3** says that Jonah was panicky about going to Nineveh, as directed by the Lord; instead he sailed to Tarshish, in the opposite direction to escape the direction of God.
-The twelve disciples were afraid. In **Matthew 8:23-27**, they are with Jesus on a boat during a storm on the Sea of Galilee, and the disciples were fearing their lives. Jesus says to them, "O, you of little faith, why are you afraid?" In other words, I (Jesus) am with you, you do not need to worry about anything, I'll take care of it!
-Peter, one of the key disciples was afraid. In **Matthew 26:69-75** Peter denies knowing Jesus three times, fearful that he might lose his life because of his association with Jesus.

<u>Prescription for Fear</u>: God wants you to know that with Him you can battle and defeat the fear within and without. Learn to GO TO GOD FIRST with any fear that you have.

1. Corrie Ten Boom was a Christian Dutch watchmaker who hid many innocent Jewish people from the Nazis during the Holocaust of World War II. In her book the *Hiding Place,* she said "Never be afraid to trust an unknown future to a known God." God wants you to *trust* Him completely.

    Psalm 56:3-4 When I am afraid, I will trust in you (God). In God, whose word I praise, in God I trust; I will not be afraid. What can mortal man do to me?

Psalm 34:4 I sought the Lord, and He answered me; He delivered me from all my fears. The angel of the Lord encamps around those who fear Him, and He delivers them.

2. Overcome the intimidation of a fear by relying on God, who has more strength and power than you can imagine. You can't escape His help if you rely on Him.

   Psalms 139:7-11 Where can I go from Your Spirit? Where can I flee from Your presence? If I go up to the heavens, You are there; if I make my bed in the depths, You are there. If I rise on the wings of the dawn, if I settle on the far side of the sea, even there Your hand will guide me, Your right hand will hold me fast. If I say, "Surely the darkness will hide me and the light become night around me," even the darkness will not be dark to You; the night will shine like the day, for darkness is as light to You.

   Psalm 105:4 Look to the Lord and His strength; seek His face always.

3. Don't run from fear. Admit that you have a problem. Commit it to God and trust Him to work with you to defeat your trepidation.

   Psalm 55:1-2 Listen to my prayer, O God, do not ignore my plea; hear me and answer me. My thoughts trouble me and I am distraught.

   Psalm 141:1 O Lord, I call to you; come quickly to me. Hear my voice when I call to You.

4. Only Jesus can take your fear of death away. The apostle Paul teaches this fact in **1 Corinthians 15:54b-55**- Death has been swallowed up in victory. Where, O death, is your victory? Where, O death, is your sting? Without God, we are feeble in death's presence. It has the final word. Only our Good Shepherd Jesus can walk with us through this gloomy valley and bring us into safety on the other side.

   Psalm 18:2 The Lord is my Rock, my fortress, and my deliverer; my God is my Rock, in whom I take refuge. His is my shield and the horn of my salvation, my stronghold.

   Psalm 20:6 Now I know that the Lord saves His anointed; He answers him from His holy heaven with the saving power of His right hand.

Memory verse for Fear:

   Psalm 86:16 Turn to me and have mercy on me; grant Your strength to your servant

8   Guilt and Shame

"God has already taken in account the wrong turns and the mistakes in your life. Quit beating yourself up and accept his mercy."

- unknown

<u>Definition</u>: Guilt is the internal distress about doing a wrong, violating a law. It is the feeling of condemnation or blame. Shame is the painful emotion caused by guilt or a shortcoming associated with strong regret.

Guilt and shame are major problems for people. Guilt is one our human drives, but we loathe having it. What does our culture think about guilt? Consider an article written by Ann Landers. Ann (real name Esther Lederer; 1918-2002) was an American advice columnist read by 90 million people in newspapers across the country between 1955 and 2002. She said this about guilt, "One of the most painful, self-mutilating, time and energy-consuming exercises in the human experience is guilt...It can ruin your day—or your week or your life—if you let it. It turns up like a bad penny when you do something dishonest, hurtful, tacky, selfish, or rotten...Never mind that it was the result of ignorance, stupidity, laziness, thoughtlessness, weak flesh, or clay feet. You did wrong and the guilt is killing you. Too Bad. But be assured, the agony you feel is normal. Remember, guilt is a pollutant, and we don't need any more of it in the world."

Now it is one thing to be "guilty" of speeding by traveling 75 MPH in a 50 MPH, being caught stealing food from a grocery store, or selling illicit drugs. This is *legal* guilt. We expect our judicial system to come into effect and pass judgment in these instances.

In this chapter, we will discuss another kind of guilt- *psychological guilt* related to shame. That is not to say that an individual may not feel guilt for a heinous crime they have committed.

Studies show that people feel guilt around six hours a week, and during that time the average adult feels guilty three times. The feeling of guilt does not go away fast, and often hangs around for about two hours. Up to 30% of people use their guilt to learn from their mistakes. This is the one way in which guilt can be a good thing.

<u>Put a check by the reason(s) for your guilt and shame (now or in the past)</u>

____Giving into a craving; usually eating something not healthy
____Doing something wrong

_____Smoking or vaping
_____Killing someone such as in abortion or war
_____For something you did not do, but wanted to
_____Saying "no"
_____Not spending enough time with parents, family, or friends
_____Breaking a diet
_____Being short or rude to someone
_____Littering
_____Cheating on a math test, or your spouse
_____Cancelling on a friend
_____Gossiping
_____Not being committed to a person or project
_____Not being perfect
_____Not exercising enough
_____Lying to friend or family member
_____Not paying attention to your health
_____Not being on time
_____Not doing enough to help someone close to you
_____You are doing better than someone else
_____Committing a sin that is unforgiven or unconfessed

How do people deal with their guilt? Several ways- 1) They minimize it and say, "It's nothing". They bury it. 2) They rationalize the activity and say, "Everybody's doing it". 3) They compromise themselves, accept it, and just lower their moral standards, 4) They criticize themselves and "beat themselves up." 5) They numb themselves up through drug use, pursuing pleasure, or over-working in restless activity to name a few. All these ways of coping with guilt are not taking care of the main problem.

Imagine the guilt of the engineers of the rocket ship *Challenger* (in photo

left). National Public Radio ran a heartbreaking interview with Robert Ebeling, one of the engineers who worked on the 1986 *Challenger* launch that resulted in the death of all seven occupants. In January 1986, Ebeling and four other engineers pleaded for the launch to be delayed; they anticipated the precise failure that would destroy the shuttle. That night, Ebeling even told his wife, Darlene, "It's going to blow up." The engineers' pleas were refused. Three weeks after the explosion, he and another engineer, since deceased, spoke to NPR (National Public Radio). The NPR article continued: Ebeling retired soon after *Challenger*. He suffered deep depression and has never been able to lift the burden of guilt. In 1986, as he watched that haunting image again on a television screen, he said, "I could have done more. I should have done more." He says the same thing today, sitting in an easy chair in the living room, his eyes watery and his face grave. The data he and his fellow engineers presented, and their persistent and sometimes angry arguments, were not enough to sway NASA officials.

Ebeling concludes he was inadequate. He did not argue the data well enough. - *Howard Berkes, "30 Years After Explosion, Challenger Engineer Still Blames Himself," NPR (1-28-16)*

There is a terrifying scene in the movie *Jurassic Park* from 1993 when Dr. Ian Malcolm and his two friends are in a jeep trying to escape an out-of-control tyrannosaurus. The driver of the jeep looks in the rearview mirror and he sees an infuriated reptile's jaw right above the words: "OBJECTS IN MIRROW MAY BE LARGER THAN THEY APPEAR." The intensity in this movie scene is incredible.

Sometimes the giant dinosaurs of our past seem to never stop trailing us. Maybe a past abortion done without thinking through the ramifications. We look in the rearview mirrors of our lives and our faults, mistakes, and sins hang over us with guilt and shame. In the book of **Philippians**, the apostle Paul grasps the paralyzing problems of the past in people's lives. In **3:1-9**, he shares how he lived a life apart from Christ, even persecuting Christians. Regret over his past could have stymied him. He says that his new relationship with Jesus empowered him to let go of his old life. It unchained him from feeling like a prisoner: "One thing I do: Forgetting what is behind and straining toward what is ahead, I press on toward the goal" (**3:13-14**). Because Christ redeems us or makes us 'new people', we do not have to let those guilt-producing problems of the past impose our direction into the future. Paul repeats this principle in **Romans 8:1a**: Therefore, there is now no condemnation for those who are in Christ Jesus. Conversely, Satan loves it when we live in the brokenness of our past.

Over many decades practicing medicine, I have witnessed many tragic deaths. Some natural, and some not. After each death, I have always asked "Why?" One of the main ethical tenets we go by as healthcare providers came from Hippocrates (460–370 BC), the famous Greek Father of Medicine. The exact phrase "First do no harm" (Latin: Primum non nocere) is a part of the original Hippocratic oath. ... another equivalent phrase is found in Epidemics, Book I, of the Hippocratic school: "Practice two things in your dealings with disease: either help or do no harm to the patient."

I admit that 'not doing harm' to our patients is virtually impossible. Because we prescribe everything from penicillin for strep throat to insulin for diabetes to Humira for Crohn's disease, there is *always* a chance for a disaster to occur because of an adverse circumstantial event *because of a medication*. Dealing with the aftermath can be guilt producing. Here are some examples: 1) While working in northeastern India, our medical clinic treated a 12 y/o girl who had severe tonsillitis with IM penicillin. ½ hour later, she died of anaphylactic shock and there was nothing we could do to help her. 2) An elderly male had a severe case of acidosis develop and eventually death after an adverse reaction to a cholesterol medication. 3) A lady died of complications of a hypoglycemic coma secondary to a low blood sugar from the use of an oral diabetic medication and 4) We had a lady who needed an emergency total colectomy because of C. difficile colitis that was so severe she had toxic megacolon. This disease was simply brought on by one dose of a common antibiotic! Believe me, there are dozens of other stories of medical disasters that I have witnessed. The balance of the good that we do never seems to quite make up for the few tragedies that have occurred along the way.

By the grace of God, I have learned to accept that fact that doctors and other practitioners are far from perfect. We have no way of telling if a terrible and riveting adverse event will happen when we prescribe a med. I tell my patients the truth. The benefits of medications far exceed the risk, but risk is never *eliminated*. We always do what we can to prevent complications of a medication. As a corollary, you don't think negatively of automobiles as a means of travel, but we must understand every time we get in a car that we can get in a head-on crash that may be life-threatening. The risk is so small, we still get in our car and drive to the grocery store. The same goes for taking medications.

Christian author Max Lucado (in photo on left) tells a story about guilt in Leadership Magazine. "Some time ago there was a  youngster who was shooting rocks with a slingshot. He could never hit his target. As he returned to Grandma's backyard, he spied her pet duck. On impulse he took aim and let it fly. The stone hit, and the duck was dead. The boy panicked and hid the bird in the woodpile, only to look up and see his sister watching.

After lunch that day, Grandma told Sally to help with the dishes. Sally responded, "Johnny told me he wanted to help in the kitchen today. Didn't you Johnny?" And she whispered to him, "Remember the duck!" So, Johnny did the dishes. What choice did he have? For the next several weeks he was at the sink often. Sometimes for his duty, sometimes for his sin. "Remember the duck," Sally'd whisper when he objected. So weary of the chore, he decided that any punishment would be better than washing more dishes, so he confessed to killing the duck. "I know, Johnny," his grandma said, giving him a hug. "I was standing at the window and saw the whole thing. Because I love you, I forgave you. I wondered how long you would let Sally make a slave out of you."

Lucado goes on to say, "Johnny'd been pardoned, but he thought he was guilty. Why? He had listened to the words of his accuser (his sister Sally). You have been accused as well. You have been accused of dishonesty, immorality, greed, anger, and arrogance. Every moment of your life, your accuser and slanderer, Satan, is filing charges against you. As he speaks, you hang your head because you have no defense. "The sentence?" Satan asks. "The wages of sin is death," explains the judge, "but in this case the death has already occurred. For this one died with Christ." Satan is suddenly silent. And you are suddenly jubilant. You realize that Satan cannot accuse you. No more dirty dishwater. No more penance. No more nagging sisters. Just like Grandma, you have stood before the judge and hear him declare, "Not guilty.""

A major producer of guilt in us is sin, which is 'missing his mark of perfection' put forth by God. God wrote the ten commandments in **Exodus 20:3-17** laid down in about 1400 B.C. to help men and women live a moral existence. A moral code is what separates man from beast. Animals care only about survival of the fittest. God's holiness and righteousness demands morality. J. Pentecost in *Life's Problems: God's Solutions* says: Guilt is the individual's response to his or her consciousness of having violated God's holiness. When we feel sorry about our rebellion of sin, we can turn to God and because of his infinite mercy, he will totally forgive us. *Forgiveness* is the healing balm for guilt.

How can we get rid of guilt in our lives the right way? The apostle Paul specifically addresses this issue in **Romans 4:6-8**. He speaks of King David who was guilty of terrible sins-adultery, murder, lying- and yet he experienced the joy of forgiveness. We too can have this joy when we 1) quit denying our guilt and recognize that we have sinned, 2) admit our guilt to God and ask for his forgiveness, and 3) let go of our guilt and believe that God has forgiven us. This can be difficult when a sin has taken root in our lives and grown over many years, when it is serious, or when it involves others. We must remember that Jesus is willing and able to forgive every sin—no matter how heinous it is. In view of the tremendous price he paid by being crucified, it is prideful to think that any of our sins are too great for him to cover. Even though our faith is weak, our conscience sensitive, and our memory haunts us, God's word declares that sins confessed are sins forgiven- read **1 John 1:9**. When we trust Christ to save us, he removes our heavy burden of trying to please him and our guilt for failing to do so.

Prescription for Guilt and Shame: God wants you to
know that with His mercy and forgiveness, you can be guilt-free. There is no sin too great for Him to handle. Freedom at last! Learn to GO TO GOD FIRST with any mental guilt that you may have and seek His blessing to move forward.

1. Recognize your guilt and why you have it. God sees your heart and knows you thoroughly, even the number of hairs on your head.

   Psalm 94:11 The Lord knows the thoughts of all of us; He knows that they are futile.

   Psalm 31:7 I will be glad and rejoice in Your love, for You saw my affliction and knew the anguish of my soul.

2. Express sorrow of why you feel guilty before God. He desires to have you go to Him in humility.

   Psalm 116:2 Because He turned his ear to me, I will call on Him long as I live.

3. God wants to free you from your prison of guilt. He doesn't want you beating yourself up forever. King David calls out to God in prayer—and so can you:

   Psalm 142:7 Set me free from my prison, that I may praise Your name.

4. Turn away from your guilt. Ask forgiveness if you have wronged someone. Go to God who loves to forgive you and forget your sin.

Psalm 19:12 God can discern our errors. He can forgive my hidden faults.

5. Keep a proper perspective: you are not perfect. You will always have sin to deal with and the guilt that may come from it.

   Psalm 130:3-4 If you, O Lord, kept a record of sins, O Lord, who could stand? But with You there is forgiveness; therefore You are feared.

Memory verse for you regarding Guilt and Shame:

   Psalm 32:5 I acknowledged my sin to You and did not cover up my iniquity. I said, "I will confess my transgressions to the Lord"- and You forgave the guilt of my sin.

9 | Loneliness

"Loneliness and the feeling of being unwanted is the most terrible poverty."

- Mother Theresa, former missionary to the poor in Calcutta, India

<u>Definition</u>: a psychological state of mind or feeling of being excluded or estranged from other people.

We are created as social and interactive creatures. That means we are relational; we need each other; and "nobody is an island". We have desires for love, acceptance, belonging, companionship, friendship with others and God. There must be a differentiation between loneliness and the terms aloneness or solitude. Loneliness is not necessarily related to the physical situations of aloneness and solitude. Here is why. Aloneness means to be separate. This is healthy sometimes; to get away. One can be alone certainly and not be lonely. There *are* loners who are perfectly happy being by themselves. Having solitude is similar. With solitude, one chooses to withdraw and be alone. It can be for a retreat, to rest, to hear from God, or to just be silent in a hectic world. This can be refreshing to mind and spirit.

<u>Put a check by the reason(s) for your loneliness (now or in the past)</u>:

____When you are excluded from a group of friends; even as children
____When your popularity diminishes
____When you suffer loss of a good friend, spouse, or pet
____When you are criticized for being different
____When as a married couple you no longer share your deepest feelings with one another; this can leave you feeling disconnected
____When you are sick in the hospital or terminally ill
____When you have a significant change, such as retirement
____When you are lonely at the top (such as CEO of a company)
____When you alienate others because of your strong opinions
____When you don't take time to enjoy others
____When you make work more important than people
____When children leave home and you are an "empty nester"
____When you are ignored because you are elderly
____When you move to a new part of the country

From 2014 to 2017 Vice Admiral Vivek H. Murthy served as the 19th Surgeon General of the United States. From this vantage point he identified one of the most lethal health crises in America today—the epidemic of loneliness. Murthy wrote: "We live in the most technologically connected age in the history of civilization, yet rates of loneliness have doubled since the 1980s. Today, over 40% of adults in America report feeling lonely, and research

suggests that the real number may well be higher. Additionally, the number of people who report having a close confidante in their lives has been declining over the past few decades."

Most people are not aware of the powerful impact that loneliness can have on their lives. The problem of isolation and loneliness can start in *childhood*. Children can be cruel growing up in "cliques" by making others feel left out and alone. If you were ever on the receiving end of being deserted, it is very hurtful. It may even lead to low self-esteem, insecurity, fear, and worry. I always felt for the third grader who never got picked to play baseball on the playground because they may be less "athletic" than others. Kids can be rude and insensitive, and they can grow up to adulthood with the same negative traits. The individual left out feels awkward, unattractive, and uninteresting. These self-image problems can be brought into adulthood. As adults, we can be "social" (energized by people) but still struggle with loneliness.

According to internet market research firm YouGov, "the social media generation is the one that feels the most alone." Their latest report details a surge in feelings of loneliness among the millennial generation, currently between the ages of 23 and 38. In their latest poll, 30 percent of millennials reported feeling lonely either always or often, compared to 20 percent of their boomer counterparts. Given that loneliness tends to trend upward as people increase in age, such an uptick among younger adults is concerning. Researchers are also interested in the question of how internet accessibility factors into the equation. Millennials are the most likely to be frequently online, so it's possible that consistent social media usage on personal devices could be contributing to feelings of loneliness.

No matter the cause, it seems that loneliness can have adverse effects on our health. It's correlated with higher blood pressure and more heart disease and increases risk of death by 26 percent.

I see the effect of loneliness frequently in my medical practice. Because 50% of my patients are over 55 years old, I take care of many older couples who have been married over 50 years. When there is a loss of a loved one (spouse) because of cancer, stroke or heart disease, loneliness of the surviving spouse can set in quickly. Despite there being adult children and grandchildren to help fill in the gaps of time, there is still hours of time every day that must be accounted for. The loss of that 'connection' leaves the individual only with good memories.

Loneliness affects many of my patients in the hospital. When people are hospitalized, they see who their *true* friends are. They may expect a lot of people to come and look in on them, but few if any come. There are many lonely hours spent in pain. Loneliness can sting as much as the illness does.

Consider the story of a recently widowed woman: "On January 5, I discovered what true loneliness was. You see, on that day my husband of over 47 years died. On that day, I felt as though I also died; yet here I was still alive. There was now a huge void in my life. Since I was still alive, I know that it meant I needed to go on. To do that, I began to look around our church congregation. I saw many widows and widowers. There were also many other members who, for one reason or another, were alone. As much as I missed the conversations with my husband, I soon realized that perhaps these others might also be starved for conversation and support. I came up with a plan. Whenever I began to feel lonely, I would call someone. Hearing the voice of a friend has helped me. If you ever find yourself feeling lonely, try these tips: 1) Read and meditate on the Psalms to find comfort in God 2) Then, pick up the phone and call someone 3) Send a card to someone and 4) Visit someone — especially those people who may be homebound or in a nursing home. By taking your mind off self and placing it on others, you will soon realize how beneficial it is."

Dallas Willard (in photo on left), a Christian philosopher (who lost his mom as a young child), wrote of a little boy whose mom had died. He was

especially sad and lonely at night. He would come into his father's room and ask if he could sleep with him. Even then, he could not rest until he knew not only that he was with his father, but that his father's face was turned toward him. "Father, is your face turned toward me now?" "Yes," his father would say. "You are not alone. I am with you. My face is turned toward you." When at last the boy was assured of this, he could rest. Dallas Willard concludes, "How lonely life can be! Oh, we can get by in life with a God who does not speak. Many at least think they do. But it is not much of a life, and it is certainly not the life God intends for us or the abundance of life Jesus came to make available." -*John Ortberg, "God is Closer than you Think"*

Even if you do everything by the book — have close, personal friendships, have a compassionate heart and care about others, the bad news is that you can still feel abandoned at times and be lonely. Even if you marry the "right person", you will experience periods of loneliness.

Jesus, at the hardest moment in his life, was deserted by his best friends, his disciples. He told them that while he was praying in the Garden of Gethsemane (**Matthew 26:36-46**) that he yearned for their faithful support. He said, "My soul is exceedingly sorrowful, even to death." What did His close friends do? They fell asleep. Jesus totally understands your loneliness. He knows what it is like to be forsaken, and he can comfort you.

We *never* have to be lonely. God is with us. God helps us in our times of loneliness. He watches us. He never leaves us. He upholds us with his righteous right hand (read **Isaiah 41:10**).

I remember growing up playing years of Little League and then Pony League baseball. Many times, my Dad would be able to come to the game and watch me play. I loved knowing my Dad was there. It gave me an inner joy and increased our bond. He had been a baseball player when he was young and could give me advice on how to play the game. Similarly, our Heavenly Father watches over and can advise us. Isn't that a secure feeling-- that you are in life *together*?

Prescription for Loneliness: God wants you to know He will give you enormous support and comfort when you go through times of loneliness. Learn to GO TO GOD FIRST during your lonely times, and He will brighten your situation like the morning dawn.

1. God understands the hurt of loneliness. He wants you to know Him as your close friend. With Him being your friend, you will never be alone.

   Psalm 73:23 Yet I am always with You; You hold me by my right hand.

   Psalm 147:5 Great is our Lord and mighty in power; His understanding has no limit.

2. God will rescue you out of your loneliness.

   Psalms 91:14-16 The Lord says, "If someone trusts Me, I will save them. I will protect My followers who call to Me for help. When My followers call to Me, I will answer them. I will be with them when they are in trouble. I will rescue them and honor them. I will give My followers a long life and show them My power to save."

3. God wants you to have joy and fulfillment even when you are experiencing loneliness.

   Psalm 86:4 Bring joy to Your servant, for to You, O Lord, I lift up my soul.

4. God wants to comfort you in your loneliness. He desires that you praise Him no matter what your circumstances.

   Psalm 119:76 May your unfailing love be my comfort, according to Your promise to Your servant.

   Psalm 68:5-6 A father to the fatherless, a defender of widows, is God in His holy dwelling. God helps the lonely in families, He leads forth the prisoner with singing

5. God will sustain you through your lonely times. Do not give up. Do not get sidetracked by your circumstances-- focus on Him.

   Psalms 51:10-12 Create in me a pure heart, O God, and renew a steadfast spirit within me. Do not cast me from Your presence or take Your Holy

Spirit from me. Restore to me the joy of Your salvation and grant me a willing spirit, to sustain me.

<u>Memory verse for you regarding Loneliness:</u>

Psalm 100:5 For the Lord is good and His love endures forever; His faithfulness continues through all generations

10 | Insecurity

"I've made peace with insecurity, because there is no security at all."

- Dick Van Dyke- famous actor and comedian (b. 1925-)

<u>Definition</u>: an uncertainty about oneself; a lack of confidence. The state of being open to danger or threat; lack of protection.

None of us like insecurity. In fact, we battle against it. We prefer comfort

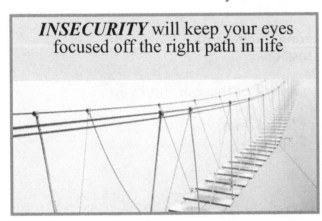

INSECURITY will keep your eyes focused off the right path in life

and refuge because it is part of our DNA to pursue security. We go for the "warm and fuzzies". That is why we like our traditions and heritage. The security of habits fights the changes that are always lurking around us. We are attracted to groups of people who provide us assurance that we are part of that group.

One of the significant areas of desired security is in our job career. We like a vocation that offers us security into the future so we can provide for our loved ones the basics of shelter and food. We like a low risk of becoming unemployed because that provides the "feeling" of security.

We do not like uncertainty. We do not like danger. We do not like threat. But we do like confidence and protection. We like reliability. We like control. We like dependability.

We like the security of a reliable car that will start every morning and bring us 25 miles to our workplace. That is despite the frigid 10 below zero temperatures outside. We 'lose it' when our car does not start! We like tight hotel security when there is a suspicious person milling around in the lobby. We like the security of having a weekend off from work every week. We know then that we can rest up to maintain our sanity.

We also desire:

-secure neighborhoods; free from violence
-secure friendships; free from disloyalty
-secure marriages; free from unfaithfulness
-secure jobs; free from stress
-secure homes; free from burglary
-secure retirements; free from financial worry

-secure states of health; free from disease
-secure nations; free from revolution and war
-secure bank accounts; free from thievery
-secure places; free from outside pressures

We love being secure, but just like Dick Van Dyke in the opening quote of this chapter, we must admit to our insecurities. There is a long list of reasons why we become unsure, emotionally fragile, and lose confidence.

Put a check by the reason(s) for your insecurity (now or in the past):

____Fear of failure
____Imperfections of appearance
____Fear of not fitting in with others
____Not measuring up to a cultural standard
____Tragedy or crisis of any kind in your life
____Rejection; being left out
____Getting significance in the wrong thing- family, job, talent,
      appearance, or material possessions
____Comparing yourself to others
____Too high of expectations for yourself or those around you
____Loss of control, or change
____Sickness or pain in yourself or loved ones
____Loss of a loved one through death
____Doubt
____Loneliness
____Being middle-aged
____Dehumanizing technology that takes over your life
____ Physical infirmities

No matter how successful one is in the worldly sense, there is still room for doubt and insecurity. Security is illusive. Look at Paul McCartney, Mike Tyson, and Jennifer Lawrence. They are candid about their lack of confidence.

In an interview with National Public Radio, Paul McCartney, celebrated Beatles' musician said this: "It seems to me that no matter how famous you are, no matter how accomplished or how many awards you get, you're always still thinking there's somebody out there who's better than you. I am often reading a magazine and hearing about someone's new record and I think, "Oh, boy, that's gonna be better than me." It's a common thing." The interviewer then asked, "But Sir Paul McCartney: You have had success in so many dimensions of music. You really feel a competitive *insecurity* with somebody else that's coming out with a record?" McCartney replied: "Unfortunately, yes ... I should be able to look at my accolades and go, 'Come on, Paul. That's enough.' But there is still this little voice in the back of my brain that goes, 'No, no, no. You could do better. This person over here is excelling. Try harder!' It still can be a little bit intimidating." *"What Makes Paul McCartney Nervous?" NPR's All Things Considered (10-15-13)*

Mike Tyson (active boxer 1985-2005; in photo on left) had worldly fame but could not conquer *insecurity*. At one time, Mike Tyson was the most feared

heavyweight boxer in the ring. Based on an interview with Tyson, Jon Saraceno revealed what went wrong: "At almost 39, he was anything but at peace. Confused and humiliated after a decadent lifestyle left him with broken relationships, shattered finances, and a reputation in ruin, the fighter could not hide his *insecurities*, stacked as high as his legendary knockouts…" "I'll never be happy," he says. "I believe I'll die alone. I would want it that way. I've been a loner all my life with my secrets and my pain. I'm really lost, but I'm trying to find myself. I'm really a sad, pathetic case." The divorced father of six was blunt, gregarious, funny, vulgar, outrageous, sad, angry, bitter, and, at times, introspective about the opportunities he squandered over the last two decades. He discussed his drug use ("The weed got me"), lack of self-esteem, and sexual addiction. He said, "My whole life has been a waste—I've been a failure." *Jon Saraceno, "Tyson: My Whole Life Has Been a Waste," USA Today (6-3-05)*

The actress Jennifer Lawrence (in photo on left), famous for her role in

The Hunger Games films, has had a long battle with *insecurity*. In a 2014 interview, she said: "In middle school there are all these peers judging you, and you're never good enough, never wearing the right outfit, saying the right thing. I wanted everyone to like me. Who doesn't? Then you grow up and become famous, and it's the same thing multiplied by a billion." When she saw herself on a recent TV program being interviewed, she had a full-fledged panic attack. Ms. Lawrence said, "All of a sudden it was like being hit by a train—this realization of how many people are looking at me, how many opinions there are." In her worst moments, she's certain her career will come crashing down. "People are going to get sick of me," she said. "I'm way too annoying. But if people want to start a backlash [against me], I'm the captain of the team. As much as you hate me, I'm ten steps ahead of you." *People magazine (5-23-14); original source: Aaron Gell, "Jennifer Lawrence Just Can't Help It".*

Look at what a high society couple did to deal with the *insecurity* that

their daughters would not be admitted to USC for college in Los Angeles, California. In March 2019, *People* magazine reported that *Full House* actress Lori Loughlin was released on a $1 million bail after surrendering to the authorities. Loughlin and her husband, fashion designer Mossimo Giannulli (who was also charged and released on bail) were charged with paying $500,000 to get their two daughters into USC by bribing coaches to designate them as athletic recruits for the crew team—despite neither girl rowing competitively. People go "all out" to battle their insecurities.

Maxwell Maltz, who wrote the book *PsychoCybernetics*, estimates that majority of people in our society have a strong sense of insecurity. Inferiority, inadequacy, and insecurity all go together. When you look at being human, you wonder how anyone feels secure. You cannot even count on your next minute or your next breath. Many circumstances are totally out of our control. You might be driving home from work today and have a head-on collision caused by an intoxicated alcoholic driver who crosses the center line. There are thousands of traffic deaths alone every year in the U.S. because of "drinking and driving". Now cell phone use is starting to catch up as a cause of countless traffic accidents. Any thinking person recognizes some degree of insecurity hour by hour of living.

Childhood influences also shape us significantly. Some people say that experiences as a youngster produce feelings of inferiority and insecurity from which we never break free from. A noted Christian psychiatrist says parents who excessively criticize their children's failures cause them to mature into adults with a warped idea of what appropriate standards are. Some parents give too little praise, thanks, and congratulations. We wonder why kids grow up to be fragile adults, always looking for comfort.

With what kind of ways do people fight their insecurity and low self-confidence? Four main ones. 1) They run away by becoming more shy and introverted- they 'clam up' 2) They become hypercritical. They criticize others by trying to bring them down to their level and make themselves look better 3) They brag a lot and become arrogant, puffing themselves up to a higher level (this is common on social media) 4) They run away and escape by diving headlong into drug use, all sorts of addictions, and authoritative rebellion.

Does God love us despite our insecurities? Without a doubt, he has a key role. After all, in his sovereignty, he allows insecurity to exist in the world. Think about it this way: God uses insecurities to point us in a positive direction *towards* him. But we must have our blinders off to see him work. He is imploring us when we are in an insecure situation: "This could be dangerous! Stay away or Beware!"

God can use insecurity to instruct us. Insecurity can tell us to take protective action. Examples: If you are at a party and walk out on a second-floor apartment terrace with eight other people, you might feel secure until you see the rotten wood in floor of the balcony. Your mind screams at you, "Get off this balcony!" If your job is going well but then you get a lousy boss who is irate most of the time, new insecurity is yelling at you, "Think about looking for

another job!" If you are a Marine on a military convoy in a Humvee driving through a village in Afghanistan and there are bombs going off around you or you are being shot at by rebels using Brown Bess smoothbore muskets, you should feel insecure and think quickly how fast you can get out of the mess! Two practical teachings of Jesus on insecurity are found in the parable of the rich man in the Gospel of **Luke 12:16-21** and secondly in the story of the House Foundations in **Matthew 7:24-27**. The theme behind these lessons is for us to seek true protection that *only* God can provide. The rich man built up quite a bit of wealth (crops and grains) for himself and wanted to build new bigger barns to house his new wealth. That way, he could relax for the next part of his life and eat, drink, and be merry. But Jesus' reply to this was straight forward. Why should he get security found in possessions and things? What if he dies tomorrow? What good are goods? The rich man died before he could use what was stored in the barns. Jesus is saying there is only insecurity in material possessions. Planning for life before death is acceptable at best, but it is much smarter to prepare for the true security you can have after death.

The story comparing the houses built on the Sand or on the Rock in **Matthew 7:24-27** is a reminder of the problem with putting value on the wrong things on this earth. A house build in muck and sand is representative of those people who find their security in *anything but* Jesus Christ and a personal relationship with Him. When conflict comes to disrupt security, depression and anxiety are the result. For the individual who has their house foundation built on the Rock (Jesus Christ), the storms of life will come and have no ill effect.

Prescription for Insecurity: God wants you to know He alone can give you ultimate security in life. Without Him, temporal security is just that; short lived. Learn to GO TO GOD FIRST when you feel insecurity, and He will give you the protection in the middle of a stormy world.

1. God gives us safety and security, and a personal relationship with Jesus gives us a peace that surpasses all understanding.

   Psalm 27:5 For in the day of trouble He will keep me safe in His dwelling; He will hide me in the shelter of His tabernacle and set me high upon a rock.

   Psalm 4:8 I will lie down and *sleep in* peace, for You alone, O Lord, make me dwell in safety

2. God is our firm foundation in times of insecurity and trouble.

   Psalm 40:2 He lifted me out of the slimy pit, out of the mud and mire; He set my feet on a rock and gave me a firm place to stand.

3. Doubt leads to insecurity. Satan loves it when you doubt God more. Trust leads to certainty. God wants trust to be the cornerstone of your life.

   Psalm 9:10 Those who know Your name will trust in You, for You, Lord, have never forsaken those who seek You.

4. Preoccupation with the things of the world lead to insecurity. Re-focus your life on God and be content in Him.

Psalm 73:24 You guide me with your counsel, and afterward You will take me into glory.

Psalm 16:5a Lord, You have assigned me my portion and my cup You have made my lot secure.

Memory verse for Insecurity:

Psalm 23:1 The Lord is my shepherd, I shall not be in want.

Psalm 108:4 For great is Your love, higher than the heavens; Your faithfulness reaches to the skies.

The **Insecurity Funnel** on page 61 is stimulated by additional Positive Stressors and additional Negative Stressors. The key: Understand that Additional STRESSORS can be either positive or negative, and both can affect us greatly.	
Some examples include:	
Positive Stressors	Negative Stressors
A new marriage	A new divorce
A new job	Being fired or let go
A new house	Being rejected by a friend
Graduating	Getting a bad grade
Having children	Deteriorating health
Quitting smoking	Grieving a death

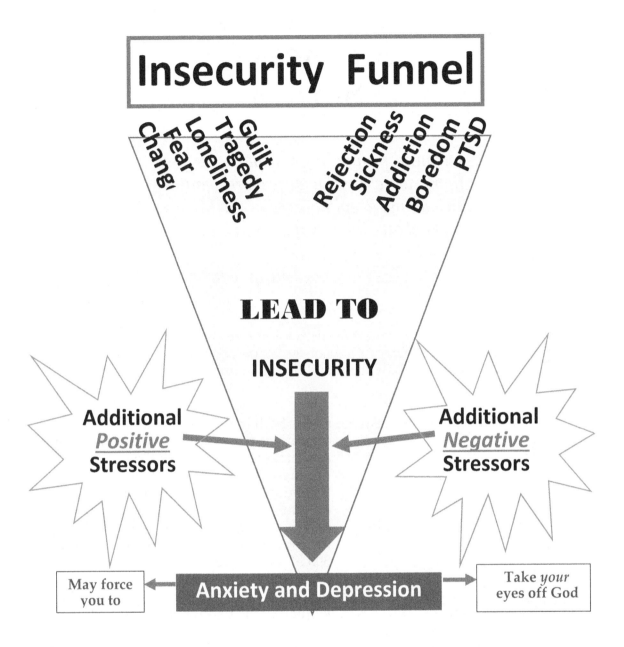

Insecurity Funnel

Guilt
Tragedy
Loneliness
Fear
Change!

Rejection
Sickness
Addiction
Boredom
PTSD

LEAD TO

INSECURITY

Additional *Positive* Stressors

Additional *Negative* Stressors

May force you to

Anxiety and Depression

Take *your* eyes off God

Ten problems in life that lead to **INSECURITY**, the main pathway in the downward spiral to **ANXIETY** and **DEPRESSION**. Don't forget about sin. It too brings us down the *slippery slope in the funnel*. Additional life stressors, positive or negative, help to accelerate the process. Our lives have different chapters depending on our age, but each chapter has its unique stressors, both *positive* and *negative*.

11   Sickness & Sorrow

"I feel helpless around people in great pain. Helpless, and guilty. I stand beside them, watching facial features contort and listening to the sighs and moans, deeply aware of the huge gulf between us. I cannot penetrate their suffering; I can only watch."

- Philip Yancey, author of 'Where Is God When It Hurts?'

<u>Definition</u>: *Pain* is the unpleasant or distressing sensation which causes suffering due to bodily injury or a disorder; acute or chronic. *Sickness* is the state of being affected with ill health; ailing with either an acute or chronic illness.

As a practicing internist who works both in the hospital and at the outpatient clinic, I have witnessed a gamut of sickness and pain over the last three decades-- cancer, strokes, heart attacks, accidents, overwhelming infections, spinal cord injuries, broken bones, kidney stones, and dozens more. 50% of the patients in my practice are over 50 years old, and over 300 of them have died in the last 5 years. Most of the time, leading up to those deaths were many lengthy illnesses. The woman in the photo here is receiving chemotherapy for lung cancer.

It is even more difficult when young people and children experience the ravages of disease. I can vividly remember while working the Congo, Africa and seeing an eight y/o boy with Tropical Splenomegaly Syndrome from repeated infections caused by a protozoan called Plasmodium (malaria). His spleen was six times normal in size and he was suffering from chronic abdominal pain. All because of mosquito bites!

I have experienced sickness and pain in my life. I have had numerous medical illnesses over the years and have been hospitalized several times and experienced the "gnashing of teeth" that can come with severe pain. I have learned that sickness and pain have purpose, even though it's hard to fathom that when you're going through the despair. I have learned that *no* person is exempt from sickness. If you have not been sick (and I mean more than just a 'cold'), then your time will no doubt come.

Sickness is in all reaches of the world; in civilized nations like the U.S. and Europe, as well as developing countries like Haiti, in cold places like Iceland and hot places like Tahiti. Men, women, and children are all prone to it. It affects all classes of people. Kings, presidents, unlearned street persons, teachers, students, doctors, janitors, construction workers, and ballerinas get attacked by this great enemy. Visit the waiting room of an ICU sometime (see photo on the left) and you will see people from all walks of life there. There are no racial or economic boundaries. The primary rope that ties people together there is the overreaching concern for a loved one who is intensively ill, maybe even dying. Some are crying and consoling others.

C.S. Lewis, British writer and lay theologian said that suffering through illness, pain, or death may be the only megaphone that can prompt people to think about the true meaning of life. Sickness halts us in our tracks and causes us a pause in a busy life. **Proverbs 18:11** says, "The wealth of the rich is their fortified city; they imagine it an unscalable wall." Even gated communities do not keep out sickness and disease.

Sickness is not preventable by anything that mankind can do. **Psalm 90:10** states, "The length of our days is seventy years---or eighty, if we have the strength, yet their span is but trouble and sorrow, for they quickly pass, and we pass away." Even are advancement in medical sciences has not impacted our lifespan. It is one thing to die at the ripe old age of 80, but how do we cope with childhood loss? How do deal with the despair of an accident or cancer that claims the life of a five y/o?

Sickness is often one of the most humbling trials that we can go through-from the soles of our feet to the crown of our heads we are susceptible to sickness. Who can count the numerous ailments that can plague us? Sometimes sickness can remove our desire to live. It can take the strongest person and turn him into a meek child feeling like "even a grasshopper is a burden" (read **Ecclesiastes 12:5**). Thousands upon thousands of diseases that affect mankind are written about a million textbooks. It has been said that research on "health-related matters" is the number one reason that people utilize the internet. Life is fragile.

The side effects of sickness and pain can reveal our misery- hopelessness and anguish. It is a true test of our endurance. Running a 26-mile marathon pales in comparison to fighting cancer or some other serious chronic condition.

Sickness is a solemn teacher for us- "Can God be a God of love and mercy when he permits miserable sickness, from AIDS to Down's syndrome to pancreatic cancer to spina bifida to coronavirus?" This is the question which often comes from the heart of people going through suffering or those watching their loved ones suffer in pain or illness. In the big picture, which people often overlook, sickness can be a *signpost* for us for the following five reasons:

1) Sickness helps to remind us of the sobering aspect of life- that there is death, even though we may not want to think about it! Many of us live as if we are never going to die. We tend to our careers, retirement accounts, hobbies, and pleasurable vacations as if earth was our eternal home. Sickness awakens us from our dreams. We should live in a way that we prepare ourselves to meet God.

2) Sickness helps us to think more thoughtfully about God, our souls, and the world to come. In **Jonah 1:5**, we see sailors in the middle of severe storm and when death was in sight being afraid and crying "every man to his god."

3) Sickness and pain help to soften hearts. The natural heart of all of us can be as hard as stone. It exposes the emptiness of the world's values and teaches us to hold them with a "loose hand." Money, a vacation home, and your retirement account are of no help to you on the hospital bed.

4) Sickness humbles us. We are all naturally proud of anything that we have accomplished in life- career building and family top the list. We secretly flatter ourselves that we are better and "not as other men." **Job 4:19** says that when we are sick, "that we can be crushed more readily than a moth." How true.

5) Sickness will try a person's religion if he or she has one. Few have a religion that will bear introspection. Most are content with their traditions and cannot find inward hope. Serious sickness often reveals a cracked foundation. It will break down when death is in sight. Jesus alone can rob death of its sting and enable us to face sickness without fear. He came to conquer the power of death.

What can we practically learn from sickness?

1) Sickness without a doubt can put us 'through the grinder". We can swear and get angry at it, or we can learn to bear it patiently. **Proverbs 16:32a** say "Better a patient man than a warrior." Learn to turn to God, your Comforter. Learn to depend on only him and others.

2) Sickness gives us who are healthy a chance to help our family, friends, and neighbors who are experiencing pain and suffering. There is a call-to-duty here. "Carry each other's burdens" (**Galatians 6:2**). Jesus was about "going about doing good" to the sick by consoling and healing (**Acts 10:38**).

3) Either you have a soul or you don't. You would likely never say you do not have a soul. The wisest man ever says that all men and women think that there is an eternal existence (**Ecclesiastes 3:11**). If you do not know Christ personally, turn to him as soon as you can and be saved forever.

4) You can glorify God in your sickness by putting yourself in God's hands. Though hard, learn to be a patient sufferer. "Be still and know that I am God" (read **Psalms 46:10**). Think about your true purpose in life.

5) Sickness forces us to be more like Jesus in experience than when we are in good health. "Jesus took our infirmities and bared our sicknesses" (**Matthew 8:17**). Jesus was a "man of sorrows and acquainted with grief" (**Isaiah 53:3**).

A few more serious sicknesses that you see, and few more funerals that you attend, and your own will take place someday. Medicines, friends, hearing, vision, earthly miracles, the power of prayer, will all eventually fail us. The world will disappear before us. Eternity will be looming large. Nothing will enable us to feel "I fear no evil" (**Psalms 23:4**) *except* a close communion with Jesus. "Cleave to Jesus more closely, love him more heartily, live for him more thoroughly, copy him more exactly, confess him more boldly, and follow him more fully."- *JC Ryle, Bishop of Liverpool England in the early 1800's.*

While we are reviewing the subject of sickness, let's discuss the broader topic of *sorrow* or *suffering.*

Our world is filled with tragedies and we experience them every day- for example, on December 26, 2004, an earthquake beneath the Indian Ocean created a *tsunami* tidal wave that caused more than 200,000 deaths on the shores of Southeast Asia. On August 29, 2005, New Orleans was hit by hurricane Katrina. Within a few hours, 80% of the city was flooded. Some of us may be in a severely unhappy marriage, or have a handicapped child from birth, or be battling the bitter disappointment of a miscarried pregnancy, or the premature loss of a loved one through the agony of a motor vehicle accident. When pain and suffering strike, people often ask, "Where is God?" This is an age-old question.

Men and women for centuries have grappled with suffering in the world. People find it difficult to accept that tragedies can be allowed by God. Why me? Why my mother? Why my son? Why? Why? Why? Let me ask you this, "Is God Santa Claus?" God gave us the book of Job in the Old Testament (written between 1800 and 2000 B.C.) to answer the difficult questions on why there is suffering in the world.

Satan and God have a conversation in the beginning of the book. A first view of suffering is from Satan. His view is shared early in the book (**Job 1:1-2:13**). He says that people believe in God *only* when they were prosperous and when life was going well for them and they are not suffering. In other words, loving God was *conditional* on being treated well by him. Satan says, "Add some suffering to people's lives and we shall see what happens." This is an "offensive slap in the face to God", as we shall discuss later.

God allows Satan to interfere in the life of the blameless and righteous "all around good guy" Job. How did Job suffer? He lost his wealth, his family, and his health. How is that for the top three categories in anyone's life?

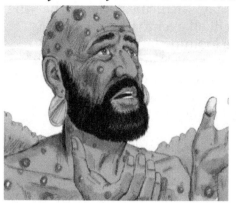

Job 1:14 Job's oxen and donkeys were carried off by his enemy the Sabeans. His servants were killed. **Job 1:16** The fire of God (lightning, see **1 Kings 18:38**) burned up the sheep and the servants. **Job 1:17** The Chaldean enemies swept down and carried off all of Job's camels. **Job 1:18-19** A mighty wind swept in from the desert and struck the four corners of the house where Job's sons and daughters were feasting. It collapsed and killed all of Job's family. **Job 2:4-7** Job is afflicted with painful sores from head to toe. See photo on left. He took a piece of broken pottery to scrape himself.

In all, Job experienced eight, painful episodes of suffering. Why? That seems rather excessive, doesn't it? You feel sorry for him, a man that didn't do anything to deserve the carnage. We go on with the story.

Job's two friends gave a second view of the cause of his suffering (see **Job 3:1-31:40**). They tell Job that his suffering was God's judgment for sin in his life. This is not always true, though sin can have its' consequences. Jesus spoke to this in **Luke 13:1-5**. Jesus instructs his people that all are sinners need to repent, or they will perish (eventually go to hell). When people seemingly suffer more, it is not necessarily related to the fact that they have sinned more. Jesus gave an example of when the tower of Siloam fell on some Galileans--that didn't happen because "they were more guilty" than anyone else. The third view of suffering was submitted by a third friend **Elihu** (see **Job 32:1-37:24**). He shared with Job that suffering was God's way to teach, discipline, and refine him. The fourth view of suffering was God's view (see **Job 38:1-41:34**). Suffering causes us to trust God for *who* He is, not *what* He does or allows to happen.

In chapters **Job 38:1-41:34**, God confronted Job with the need to be content (though perhaps difficult) without knowing why he was suffering. God didn't explain the reason for the pain. Instead, God gave Job a lesson on the amazing facts of nature, and that He was in control of it all. From sunrises, to rain, snow, thunderstorms, creatures, birds, etc., God declares his satisfaction with all of it. "Do you, Job, still want to argue with the Almighty (**40:2**)?" Job's response to God- "I was talking about things I did not understand" (**42:3-5**). Did God specifically answer Job about the reason for his suffering and pain? Not really. Phillip Yancey, in his book, "Where Is God When It Hurts?" says this, "God's message to us about suffering is this: Until you know a little more about running the physical universe, don't tell God how to run the moral universe. Until we are wise enough to orchestrate a blizzard—or even manufacture a single perfect snowflake—we have no grounds to berate God. Let him who is about to accuse God consider the greatness of the God accused."

Jesus acknowledged God's control over his life despite all the suffering that he was going through for us. It is the ability of God to arrange human events to fulfill his purposes that makes his sovereignty incredible and yet mysterious. Just as God's rule over our lives is invincible, so it is incomprehensible. **Isaiah 55:9** says, "His ways are higher than our ways," and **Romans 11:33** says, "His judgments are unsearchable, and his paths are beyond tracing out." God's plan for us is much bigger for our lives than we can know. He must have faith in this fact. If not, the rejection of God will likely follow.

We can be comforted because God comforts us in our suffering. **2 Corinthians 1:56** says, "For just as the sufferings of Christ flow over into our lives, so also through Christ our comfort overflows. If we are distressed, it is for your comfort and salvation; if we are comforted, it is for your comfort, which produces patient endurance of the same sufferings we suffer."

When God comforts us, our troubles do not always go away! If this were always so, people would turn to the Lord only out of desire to be relieved from pain and not out of love for him. Being comforted can mean receiving encouragement and hope to deal with our trouble.

As Christian's, God can make "good" out of suffering. The Bible clearly teaches this. **Acts 5:41**-The apostles rejoiced because they had been counted worthy of suffering disgrace for the name of Christ. **Acts 8:1-9-** God can take suffering (the stoning of Stephen), and make good from it. This tragic event fired up the believers to evangelize. **Romans 5:2b-** We rejoice in our sufferings, because we know that suffering produces perseverance, perseverance, character; and character, hope. And hope does not disappoint us, because God has poured out his love into our hearts by the Holy Spirit. **Romans 8:17-** As Christians, we share in his sufferings in order that we may also share in his glory. Finally, God took the awfulness of the crucifixion and made it good-so that all his creation could be redeemed for eternal life.

During World War II, the Ten Boom family exemplified a steadfast trust in God's control of their lives, despite their suffering. After their beloved Holland was overrun by Nazis, the Ten Booms rescued an estimated *800 Jewish people* in 18 months. The Nazis eventually arrested the Ten Booms and sent them to concentration camps. Corrie ten Boom alone lived to talk about it (in photo on the left). She endured unspeakable suffering and watched her sister Betsie die. After the war, Corrie traveled the world speaking about her experiences and how the gospel enabled her to forgive her enemies. She was able to forgive the Nazis.

Corrie often used the example of a tapestry to demonstrate God's control in our lives. The underside may appear like a knotted mess. But the front reveals a beautiful design. One day we will see from God's perspective how he was sculpting our lives, even though it seemed messy at times. Corrie lived with certainly because she believed in God's sovereignty.

God's work in our lives may involve chastening and times when he seems silent and hidden. But because of his promises, we can rest in his control, comfort, and appropriate his matchless grace. - *"Israel My Glory"* magazine, Jan/2017.

We may experience affliction that feels endless, situations that appear desperate, or waiting that seems unbearable. We may endure moments when the odds against us are stacked against us. We may not experience the healing we long for. Be we trust in him and never give up hope. We believe that he is always able, always trustworthy, and always present. As Phillip Yancey says,

"Where is God when it hurts? He is in us—not in the things that hurt—helping to transform bad into good."

In *Our Daily Bread*, David Fisher tells a poignant story of Jean-Dominique Bauby, who overcame the odds of severe suffering to write a book entitled, "*The Diving Bell and the Butterfly*". Bauby had a massive stroke leaving him with a condition call "Locked-In Syndrome". Although he was almost completely paralyzed, Bauby was able to write his book by blinking his left eyelid. An aide would recite a coded alphabet, until Bauby blinked to choose the letter of a word he was dictating. The book required about 200,000 blinks to write. He used the only physical ability left him to communicate with others.

In 2 Timothy, the apostle Paul was "locked-in". Under house arrest, he learned that his execution might be soon. With this in view, he said, "I suffer trouble…even to the point of chains; but the Word of God is not chained"- **2 Timothy 2:9**. In spite of his isolation and suffering, Paul welcomed visitors, wrote letters of encouragement, and rejoiced at the spread of God's word. If circumstances have isolated you from others such as being in a hospital bed, serving time in a prison, or being a shut-in, look up! Reflect on some ways you can still reach out to others.

Prescription for Pain, Sickness, and Suffering: God wants you to know you can have hope, encouragement and comfort during your pain and sickness. Learn to GO TO GOD FIRST when you have sickness or pain, because He understands what you are going through.

1. God knows what you are going through. He understands your hurts. He has not abandoned you or forgotten you. He wants to heal you. When you have a sickness or significant pain, it can bring on frustration because you feel you have lost control of what's going on in your life.

   Psalm 6:2 Be merciful to me, Lord, for I am faint; O Lord, heal me, for my bones are in agony. My soul is in anguish. How long, O Lord, how long?

   Psalm 147:3 God heals the brokenhearted and binds up their wounds.

2. Jesus, the Son of God, went through great suffering Himself. And it is Jesus who comes to strengthen and comfort you in your trouble.

   Psalms 59:16-17 I will sing of Your (God's) strength, in the morning I will sing of Your love; for You are my fortress, my refuge in times of trouble. O my Strength, I sing praise to You; You, O God, are my fortress, my loving God.

3. God is close to your through your illness and pain.

   Psalm 34:18 The Lord is close to those who have suffered disappointment. He saves those who are discouraged.

4. It is true that God does not always prevent sickness and pain in his children. It is through His sufferings, not ours, that we are made right with Him. He uses even our pain and suffering for our ultimate good.

    Psalms 9:9-10 Many people are suffering-crushed by the weight of their troubles. But the Lord is a refuge for them, a safe place they can run to. Lord, those who know Your name come to You for protection…You do not leave them without help.

5. You forget our years of good health after a few days of illness. You quickly forget our years of freedom after a few days of being in the hospital. Thankfulness drains away along with decreasing strength. Learn to wait on the Lord during your difficult time.

    Psalm 34:1-3 I will praise the Lord all the time. I will never stop singing His praises. Humble people, listen and be joyful, while I brag about the Lord. Praise the Lord with me. Let us honor His name.

Memory verse for Sickness & Suffering:

Psalm 40:1 I called to the Lord, and He heard me. He heard my cries. He lifted me out of the grave. He lifted me from that muddy place.

12 Post-Traumatic Stress

"In World War I, they called it shell-shocked. Second time around (WWII), they called it battle fatigue. After Vietnam, they called it Post-Traumatic Stress Disorder"

- Jan Karon, American novelist

<u>Definition</u>: PTDS (Post-Traumatic Stress Disorder) is a condition of on-going mental stress occurring as a result of injury or previous psychological shock, typically involving sleep disturbance and recurrent, vivid *memories* of the experience, with a resultant dulled response to the outside world.

It is estimated that 70 % of adults in the U.S. have experienced some type of traumatic event at least once in their lives—that is over 200 million people! An estimated 8 percent of Americans -- 24.4 million people - have PTSD at any given time. An estimated 1 out of 10 women develops PTSD; women are about *twice* as likely as men to get PTSD.

PTSD develops in about 1 in 3 people who experience severe trauma. It's not fully understood why some people develop the condition while others do not. Certain factors appear to make some people more likely to develop PTSD. If you have had depression or anxiety in the past, or do not receive support from family or friends, you're more susceptible to developing PTSD after a traumatic

event. There may also be a genetic factor involved in PTSD. For example, having a parent with a mental health problem is thought to increase your chances of developing the condition. With PTSD comes a cascade of possible fear, anxiety, low self-esteem, anti-social behavior, depression, or emotional lability.

Most people that I see with PTSD in my medical practice have had a very scarring experience in the past while in the armed forces. The event often involves killing the enemy. Back in the 1980's, I saw men with PTSD who fought in the Battle of the Bulge in World War II. Since then, other military conflicts including Korea, Vietnam, and Iraq have yielded their share of victims of PTSD. But there are many other reasons for PTSD.

<u>Put a check next to the reason(s) you have experienced PTSD</u>:

_____War conflicts, with exposure to extreme violence

____ Physical or sexual assault (especially rape)
____ Abuse, including domestic or childhood
____ Exposure to traumatic events at work (such as an irate boss)
____ Serious accidents with associated pain (i.e. bad falls)
____ Childbirth experiences, such as losing a baby
____ A frightening event; past or present (being badly bitten by a dog)
____ Serious health problems; including an ICU admission
____ Torture (such as in being a POW)
____ Being in prison (experiencing the brutality of other prisoners)
____ Having a traumatic relationship of any kind

Studies have shown that people with PTSD have abnormal levels of stress hormones. Normally, when in danger, the body produces higher levels of stress hormones like adrenaline to trigger a reaction in the body. This reaction, often known as the "fight or flight" reaction, helps to deaden the senses and dull pain. People with PTSD have been found to continue to produce high amounts of fight or flight hormones even when there's no danger. It's thought this may be responsible for the numbed emotions and hyperarousal experienced by some people with PTSD.

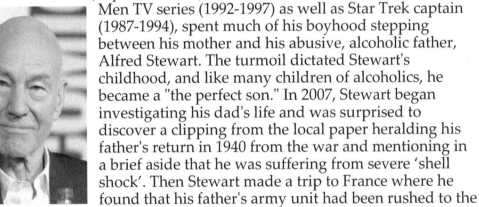

Patrick Stewart (in photo on left), the British-born actor and star of the X-Men TV series (1992-1997) as well as Star Trek captain (1987-1994), spent much of his boyhood stepping between his mother and his abusive, alcoholic father, Alfred Stewart. The turmoil dictated Stewart's childhood, and like many children of alcoholics, he became a "the perfect son." In 2007, Stewart began investigating his dad's life and was surprised to discover a clipping from the local paper heralding his father's return in 1940 from the war and mentioning in a brief aside that he was suffering from severe 'shell shock'. Then Stewart made a trip to France where he found that his father's army unit had been rushed to the front as the Germans slashed through France. Alfred Stewart and his men were caught between a marsh and a bridge, pinned down by bombing for hours. The train conductor had uncoupled the engine and drove away, leaving the troops stranded. Alfred Stewart and his men spent the next month on the run from the Germans before being evacuated. Then, despite his shell-shocked status, Alfred Stewart volunteered for the paratroopers. During August 1944 he played a significant role in the liberation of England that he had watched crumble four years earlier. Patrick Stewart, who knew nothing about his father's military heroism and agony, said, "I was brought face-to-face with the knowledge that he was a man with experiences I was unaware of … There were reasons why he was an alcoholic and depressed at times. I've talked to people who understand post-traumatic stress disorder and described my father's behavior, and they've said, 'Absolutely classic PTSD behavior! No doubt about it.'" After hearing the real story of his father's life, Patrick said, "My anger toward him completely dissolved."

PTSD can induce worry, depression, a low self-image, and panic. A 50 y/o patient has suffered from PTSD for over 20 years related to the death of her daughter born 5 ½ months premature. The daughter was in the NICU for 3 ½ months before finally being discharged. The first night home, her tiny daughter had a respiratory arrest and was transported back to the hospital by ambulance. Unfortunately, she expired because of a lack of brain oxygen after 8 days of hospitalization. Mom got moral support from her family and friends and counseling in those initial days and months. Despite this excellent provision, she continued to fight the feelings of guilt and blame for years. Her PTSD symptoms would sometimes surface as flashbacks when she heard any ambulance's sirens blaring. Then in 2018, the Lord drew her close to himself and she experienced a resurgence of her faith in him. She finally started to win the battle against PTSD—once and for all she was been given freedom from guilt and shame. She gave her burdens to him and he has gladly comforted her.

Mike Wittmer in 'Our Daily Bread' (*12/2019*) tells a story about an accomplished writer named Caitlin who described her PTSD and depression since fighting off a physical assault. The emotional violence cut deeper than her physical struggle, for she felt it proved "how undesirable she was." "I was not the kind of girl you wanted to get to know," she said. She felt unworthy of love and devalued. Mike goes on to say that despite our feelings of unworthiness and feeling undervalued, Jesus understands us. Jesus wasn't only betrayed by one of his 12 disciples Judas Iscariot. He was betrayed with contempt. The Jewish leaders despised Christ, so they offered Judas 30 pieces of silver-the lowest price you could put on a person, the price put on a slave. Judas thought so little of Jesus he sold him for nearly nothing. If people undervalue Jesus, don't be surprised when they undervalue you. Your value isn't in what others do or say. It's entirely and only what God says, and he thinks you are worth dying for!

In a 2009 article in Christianity Today magazine, author Jocelyn Green  gave readers a glimpse into the lives of different military officers suffering from post-traumatic stress disorder-- with special attention given to the responsibility the church has in ministering to those officers. She writes this: "Nate Self's military record was impeccable. A West Point graduate, he led an elite *US Army Ranger* outfit and established himself as a war hero in March 2002 for his leadership during a 15-hour ambush firefight in Afghanistan. The battle resulted in a Silver Star, a Purple Heart, and a position as President Bush's guest of honor for the 2003 State of the Union. But by late 2004, he walked away from the Army. In another surprise attack, post-traumatic stress disorder (PTSD) had taken his life captive. "I just hated myself," says Self. "I felt like I was somebody different. And since I did not feel like I could be who I was before, and hated who I was now, I just wanted to kill the new person. I felt like I had messed up everything in my life. The easiest way, the most cowardly way to escape, was to just depart." ..."If people think the VA hospital will solve all the problems, they'll overlook the greatest source of healing in any situation: Jesus," says Self. "The majority component for recovery is a spiritual solution, more than any secular clinical answer."

Those who suffer from PTSD continue to react, sometimes more intensely than ever, to a traumatic or life-threatening event even after the danger is past. Two out of three marriages in which one spouse has PTSD fail.

The suicide rate among those with PTSD is almost twice the national average. For example, suicide rates were up in all the armed services in 2008, with 125 confirmed suicides in the Army alone—the most the Army has seen since it started keeping records.

Prescription for Post-Traumatic Stress (Disorder):

God wants you to know he can eliminate from your mind and heart of past traumatic memories that harm you today. Learn to GO TO GOD FIRST every day in your battle against the past trauma.

1. PTSD is not a life sentence! First acknowledge that the trauma is real and impacted you in the past. Seek God for help.

   Psalm 14:2 The Lord looks down from heaven to see if there are any who seek God

   Psalm 16:6 I have set the Lord always before me. Because He is at my right hand, I will not be shaken.

2. Recognize the source of the trauma. Seek God's wisdom to help deal the psychological effects and negative memories of the trauma.

   Psalms 69:16-17 Answer me, O Lord, out of the goodness of Your love; in Your great mercy turn to me. Do not hide Your face from Your servant; answer me quickly, for I am in trouble.

   Psalms 25:4-5 Show me Your ways, O Lord, teach me Your paths; guide me in Your truth and teach me, for You are God my Savior, and my hope is in You all day long.

3. Release the triggers of the PTSD. God can deliver you from these mental triggers.

   Psalm 107:14 He brought them out of darkness and the deepest gloom and broke away their chains.

4. On the road to recovery, journal day by day, and self-examine yourself and discover the walls you have built around yourself. Seek God daily. Don't forget Him.

   Psalms 31:2-3 Turn Your ear to me, come quickly to my rescue; by my rock of refuge, a strong fortress to save me. Since You are my Rock and my fortress, for the sake of Your name lead and guide me.

   Psalm 71:5 For You have been my hope, O Sovereign Lord, my confidence since my youth

5. You are not alone in the world. You can find freedom from your past or present trauma! Know that God loves you and can lift you up with help.

    Psalm 63:7 Because You are my help, I sing in the shadow of Your wings.

Memory verses for Post-Traumatic Stress Disorder:

Psalms 89:1-2 I will sing of the Lord's great love forever; with my mouth I will make Your faithfulness known through all generations. I will declare that Your love stands firm forever, that You established Your faithfulness in heaven itself.

13 Stress

"It's not the load that breaks you down, it's the way you carry it."

- Lou Holtz, former head college football coach

<u>Definition</u>: A state of mental or emotional strain or tension resulting from adverse or demanding circumstances.

Stress comes from *inside* or from *outside* influences. By inside, I mean self-imposed. Sometimes, stressors that are very real can be exaggerated because of how we *respond* to them. Outside variables that affect you can be controlled or not controlled.

An example of a controlled variable is getting pregnant. For example-

Pregnancy can bring on more stress

you get married and you and your husband decide to have your first child. Like 83% of other couples who choose to have a child, you get pregnant in the next few months. Little did you know what you were getting in to. By getting pregnant, you open an array of uncontrollable stressors. As the Mom, your body changes. You get physically ill for the first 3 months of the pregnancy. You have pain in your lower back. Your moods change because of hormones. You fret about your baby. Will the baby be ok? You stress about the delivery. Will you handle it well? You stress about what obstetrician will deliver the baby. That will be the most important time in your life, and you want someone special to carry out the procedure. You stress about the sex of the baby (because of five siblings, you are the only girl). The list continues to grow. Here you purposely get pregnant (a controlled variable), but then you are blindsided by dozens of uncontrollable stresses along the way for the next nine months. You did not realize that the joy of bringing a beautiful baby into the world can produce some very real challenges.

Getting pregnant is but a small example of what happens to us as we experience life in the young motherhood years. How about the husband? What happens to his mental state when he finds that his wife is pregnant? After the joy of knowing he will be a Dad, he stresses about how he can help support his wife during her difficult pregnancy. He too stresses about the health of their future baby. He stresses about his ability to help with the baby since he works night shift 60 hours every week. He stresses about his ability to financially provide for his young family.

Every day in your life will expose different stresses. As we age, the chapters of our lives change, but stress does not. Some of those stressors are positive, like bringing a baby into the world. Some of the stressors will be negative. Review the different stressors in the "Insecurity Funnel" in the previous chapter on Insecurity.

When people go through a stressful situation, they can experience any of the following:

-initial disbelief and shock
-sadness, frustration (or anger), or helplessness
-difficulty with concentration or getting through the day
-psychosomatic problems such as headaches, chest pains, skipped heart beats, diarrhea
-a desire to escape by turning to nicotine, alcohol, and other drugs

I remember as a young physician consoling a 78 y/o woman in my office one day. We were in the middle of the office examination, when out of the blue, tears welled up in her eyes. Asking what was wrong, she told me that day (August 3rd) was the birthday of her young daughter Debbie who died a tragic death from acute leukemia when she was 4 years old. Here we were, fifty years later, and my sweet patient was experiencing vivid grief of her daughter's death at such a young age. From her purse, she pulled a picture (in photo on left) of her beautiful and vivacious blond-haired daughter and just sobbed. The stress of that separation had never left her.

Common causes of Stress depend on your decade of life:

Ages:

5-10 Figuring out performance in school and how to study and read. Being bullied, not fitting in, social integration with other children, building friendships, peer pressure, sibling rivalry

11-20 Dealing with your self-image, dating, social interactions, puberty (hormone changes and body changes), school performance, peer pressure, independent thinking

21-30 Marriage, starting a family, buying a house, more independence, figuring out direction in life, job performance

31-40 Growing family needs, financial stressors, learning dynamics in mixed families, learning balance between family and job

41-50 Mentoring teenagers, coping with the busyness of life, financial stressors. Finding balance.

51-60 Being grandparents or having adult children, having an "empty nest", dealing with an aging body, aches and pains and other illnesses related to aging

61-70 Dealing with ongoing aging issues, helping care for aging parents and grandchildren. The more the grandchildren, the more the stress. Having a balance in life.

71-80 Growing lists of infirmities, retirement issues, losses of friends and other family members.

81-90 Loneliness, boredom, loss of independence.

Stress about lack of money is always on the top of "Stressor Lists". A 2015 "Stress in America" survey done by the American Psychological Association (APA) shows that stress about money and finances is prevalent nationwide, even as aspects of the U.S. economy have improved. In fact, regardless of the economic climate, money has consistently topped Americans' list of stressors since the first "Stress in America" survey in 2007. Here are the highlights:

- 72% of adults report feeling stressed about money at least some of the time and 22 percent say that they experience extreme stress
- 26% of adults report feeling stressed about money most or all the time.
- Causes of money-related stress include paying for unexpected expenses, paying for essentials, and saving for retirement.
- 32% of adults say that their finances or lack of money prevent them from living a healthy lifestyle.
- 12% of Americans have said they skipped going to the doctor in the past year when they needed health care because of financial concerns. This is an unfortunate reality.

The other major stress problem for Americans is balancing work with family. A study from 2010 explored the impact of our work habits on family life in detail. The study reported, "Americans consider a 40-hour work week as

'part time' in most professional jobs and as a sign of a stagnant career." The report continued: Work-family conflict is much higher in the U.S. than elsewhere in the developed world. One reason is that Americans work longer hours than workers in most other developed countries, including Japan, where there is a word, *karoshi*, for "death by overwork". The typical American middle-income family put in an average of 11 more hours a week in 2006 than it did in 1979. As you might expect, work-life imbalance creates a lot of stress for many

U.S. families. In 2008, 42 percent of employees reported experiencing "some" or "a lot" of interference between work and family. Moreover, in recent years:

- 73 percent of mothers and 41 percent of fathers complain that they are multitasking "most of the time."
- 69 percent of mothers and 68 percent of fathers say they have "too little time" with their spouse.
- 53 percent of mothers and 37 percent of fathers report "always feeling rushed." - *David Edmund Gray, Practicing Balance (The Alban Institute, 2012)*

Healthy ways to deal with stressors of all kinds are to:

-Eat a balanced diet. Stay away from excess fat and carbohydrates- this is of utmost importance in your body dealing with stress
-Exercise regularly
-Talk to God through prayer, friends and family, about your stress
-Take a break. Develop a recreational habit so you can re-create peacefulness in your mind
-Avoid drug use- nicotine, alcohol, marijuana, cocaine, and others
-Recognize the stress that is trying to control or imprison you- parents must be perceptive of stresses their children are going through in order help support them

David H. Roper tells the story of one of his sons, Brian, who was a high school basketball coach. One year, his team was participating in the Washington State Basketball Tournament, and well-meaning folks from his hometown asked him, "Are you going to win it all this year?" Both players and coaches felt the stress and pressure, so his son adopted the motto: "Play with joy!" The idea was to enjoy the ride and opportunity, and let God take care of the rest. David went on to say that despite the daily stresses of life, sometimes discouraging news, or health problems. God can give us a *joy* that transcends these conditions if we ask him. We can have what Jesus called, "my joy" (read **John 15:11**).

Prescription for Stress: God wants you to know He can come along side you and help you with *any* stressors in your life. Learn to GO TO GOD FIRST in your struggle with stress.

1. The sooner that you learn that you cannot control the world around you, the better you will be able to cope with stress. Understand that God is in control, He is in charge over everything that happens.

   Psalms 86:8-10 Among the gods there is none like You, O Lord; no deeds can compare with yours. All the nations You have made will come and worship before You, O Lord; they will bring glory to Your name. For You are great and do marvelous deeds; You alone are God.

Psalms 109:21-22 But you, O Sovereign Lord, deal well with me for Your name's sake; out of the goodness of Your love, deliver me. For I am poor and needy, and my heart is wounded within me.

2. Regarding your specific stress, magnify your prayers to God. God wants to hear from you so He can guide your steps.

   Psalm 4:1 Answer me when I call to you, O my righteous God, give me relief from my distress; be merciful to me and hear my prayer.

   Psalm 70:5 Yet I am poor and needy; come quickly to me, O God. You are my help and my deliverer; O Lord, do not delay.

3. No matter what stresses that you have in day to day life, God can lift you up and give you joy that rises above the situation.

   Psalm 145:4 The Lord upholds all those who fall and lifts up all who are bowed down.

4. Find a good mentor to help you go through your stresses. First go to God, the greatest mentor and counselor of all, for His advice on handling stress.

   Psalm 16:7 I will praise the Lord, who counsels me; even at night my heart instructs me.

5. Despite life's unpredictable ups and down, we are grounded in the fact that God is *with us* through the turmoil, and He gives us a peace that surpasses all understanding (read **Philippians 4:6-7**)

   Psalm 14:5b God is present in the company of the righteous.

Memory verse for Stress:

   Psalm 16:5a Lord, you have assigned me my portion and my cup You have made my lot secure.

14 | **Burnout**

"I think the best piece of advice for me was when I talked to some of the great players who have had success in this league how much they emphasized the importance of rest, that you can't just go 100 miles an hour all 12 months of the year every day and just keep going. That is a recipe for burnout."

- Kirk Cousins, NFL quarterback, 2019

<u>Definition</u>: The exhaustion of physical or emotional strength or motivation usually as the result of prolonged stress or frustration.

Though we often use the term "burnout" in relation to job problems, it can be related to a myriad of other situations which produce tiredness, fatigue, and exhaustion. Exhaustion may be physical, mental, or both. Burnout is what happens to us when we simply "hit the wall". For example, J.M. is a 70 y/o male who confided in me at the office that he is struggling with burnout. He has been retired for 5 years, but unfortunately in the middle of his retirement has been diagnosed with not only breast cancer, but also Type 2 Diabetes. "This really isn't what I was expecting to be doing in my golden years," he confided. "I feel burned out. It seems like all that I do is go to doctor's offices over the last six months, and I am getting very tired of it!" "I go from the lab for blood work to the radiology department for x-rays, to the infusion center for cancer treatment, to the endocrinologist for adjustment of my medications. I feel like I am in a grind." He was not only emotionally drained but physically tired.

The spectrum of Burnout is this:

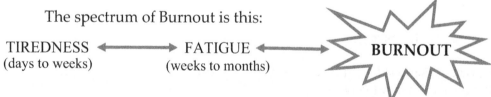

TIREDNESS ⟷ FATIGUE ⟷ **BURNOUT**
(days to weeks)   (weeks to months)

What starts as tiredness ends in burnout over a given period. But burnout can cause more fatigue, therefore causing a vicious circle. J.M.'s original stamina and attitude at the beginning of his health battles was one of, "I'm going to battle these illnesses with all I've got and *NEVER GIVE UP*." This phrase was coined by cancer fighter Jimmy Valvano back in the 1990's, who died at age 46 from metastatic adenocarcinoma. He was college basketball player, coach at North Carolina State University, broadcaster, and inspiration for us all. Over time, our body, mind, and spirit does wear down, and we can succumb to the ravages of disease, as serious illness sometimes takes no prisoners.

<u>Put a check next to the reason(s) for your Burnout (now or in the past)</u>:

____Lack of control becomes a constant
____Self-reliance
____Overwhelming demands placed on us by others or ourselves
____Repetitive experiences that become mundane (boredom)
____Lack of refreshment or breaks
____Lack of support from loved ones
____Excessive overload of health issues
____Imbalance in life; heavy workload
____Trying to be everything to everyone; saying "Yes" all the time
____Too much work, not enough play
____Lack of proper sleep, nutrition, exercise
____Pursuing the gods of money and worldly success

As our bodies mature and age, we may be even more prone to burnout when it comes to performing physical endeavors. That can be anything to walking up three flights of stairs to mowing the lawn with a push mower. Once we are over 60 years of age (and this age can be variable depending on our life experiences and genetics), our bodies wear out. Our vision starts to deteriorate, our hearing declines, our skin changes elasticity (see picture comparing a young hand to the hand of a 75 y/o on the left), our joints start aching, our muscles lose muscle mass, and our bones thin out.

Tiredness and fatigue over weeks to months are common problems for my patients. It is imperative for me to examine their lives carefully. My experience has led me to believe that 90% of chronic fatigue is related to mental weariness- such as anxiety or depression. I look for physiological causes of the rest of the 10%. We rule out medication side effects, heart problems, metabolic issues like diabetes, anemia, new liver dysfunction, electrolyte disturbance, thyroid conditions, and sleep disturbance such as obstructive sleep apnea. Rarer difficulties include hidden cancer, adrenal disturbance, or neurological problems such as myasthenia gravis. If we can find the medical reason for the fatigue, it can often be remedied with appropriate treatment. If not, and the fatigue lasts long enough, burnout is sure to follow.

Consequences of Burnout:

-excessive stress when ignored
-lack of satisfaction in life
- more fatigue making burnout worse
-insomnia or fitful sleep
-anger, irritability, sadness
-psychosomatic illness- migraines, spastic colon
-high blood pressure
-excessive eating or not eating enough

-pessimistic outlook
-low resistance to illness
-lower productivity
-apathy- "don't care" attitude
-self-doubt- loss of self-confidence
-social withdrawal

Dealing with burnout is wise because otherwise you will find yourself in a funk for a long time. It's not bad to get tired. Any good physical exercise or work will do that. It's O.K. to get fatigued for a time. But the whole process gets "out of whack" when we continue down the spiral into burnout.

Srinivasan S. Pillay, a psychiatrist and an assistant clinical professor at Harvard Medical School who studies burnout, recently surveyed 72 senior leaders and found that nearly all of them reported at least some signs of burnout and that all of them noted at least one cause of burnout at work. The article quoted one chief executive for a multibillion-dollar company who put it this way: "I just felt that no matter what I was doing, I was always getting pulled somewhere else. It seemed like I was always cheating someone—my company, my family, myself. I couldn't truly focus on anything—I was just getting burned out." - *Tony Schwartz and Christine Porathmay, "Why You Hate Work," The New York Times Sunday Review (5-30-14)*

If work is a major burnout problem for you, then the answer is to readdress your priorities. When you have a load of work to do and it matches your capabilities, then you can effectively accomplish what you set out to do day to day. You take the proper regular rest and relaxation, and that helps you to get your "batteries charged" for the next day. You even find time for professional growth and development. When you feel overloaded, and your circuits are buzzing, then balance doesn't exist and you are headed for trouble. You need to do the following: a) plan your workload b) prioritize your work c) delegate tasks d) learn to say "No" and importantly e) let go of trying to be perfect.

A long-standing pastor of a megachurch in the Midwest shared with his congregation the problem of personal burnout that had affected his ability to lead the church. Having been raised by a workaholic father, he followed in his Dad's mode of attacking his career head on. After 15 years of ministry, he realized that his life lacked the necessary balance to fight against burnout. One of his answers was to develop the hobby of sailing. Over time, he was able to navigate his sailboat for hours at a time on lakes in the area. It was when he was alone with God that he was able to not only recreate but re-create his passion for the people at his church.

Amy Boucher Pye tells the story of a woman named Emma who one spring after a dreary winter during which she helped a family member through a long illness, she found encouragement each time she walked past a cherry tree near her home in Cambridge, England. Bursting out at the top of the pink blossoms grew blossoms of white. A clever gardener had grafted into the tree a branch of white flowers. When Emma passed the unique tree, she thought of Jesus's words about being the Vine and his followers the branches in **John 15:1-8**. By calling himself the Vine, Jesus was saying that he gives sustenance and life to the branches. And as they remained in Him, receiving his nourishment and strength, they would bear fruit (**John 15:5**). As Emma supported her family member, to prevent burnout, she needed the reminder that she was connected to Jesus. Seeing the white flowers among the pink ones on the cherry tree gave her a visual truth that as she remained on the Vine, she gained the strength necessary to persist in her faith.

Anyone who has struggled with burnout for any period knows that it is something they never want to experience again. Fortunate for us, Jesus knew that we would have to go to war against burnout. He tells us in **Matthew 11:28-30**, "Take my yoke upon you and learn from me, for I am gentle and humble in heart, and you will find rest for your souls. For my yoke is easy and my burden is light." Jesus provides rest for our souls and boundaries for our schedules. God thought so much about the importance of rest that he rested on the seventh day of creation. The fourth of the Ten Commandments (**Exodus 20:8-11**) tells us to "Remember the Sabbath and keep it holy." The importance of rest so that you can focus on God can not be underestimated.

Prescription for Burnout: God wants you to know you can find refreshment in Him, the great Redeemer, Restorer, Reconciler, and Revitalizer. Learn to GO TO GOD FIRST when you are burning (or burned) out.

1. Find refreshment in God by focusing on Him first. He may also lead you to medical support, counseling, and altering your life activities.

    Psalms 46:10a Be still and know that I am God

    Psalm 32:8 I will instruct you and teach you in the way you should go; I will counsel you and watch over you.

2. Be encouraged by God. Talk with Him while you go on walks and enjoy the nature around you. Find more time for your family and pets.

    Psalms 10:17-18 You hear, O Lord, the desire of the afflicted; You encourage them, and You listen to their cry, defending the fatherless and the oppressed, in order that man, who is of the earth, may terrify no more.

3. Fight burnout by turning away from self-reliance. Learn to lean on your majestic and powerful God. He wants your burdens. They are light for him. He is God. You aren't.

    Psalms 96:5-6 For all the gods of the nations are idols, but the Lord made the heavens. Splendor and majesty are before Him; strength and glory are in His sanctuary.

    Psalm 89:17 For God is our glory and strength

4. Improve in your self-care. Take care of your health so that you can be in top-notch shape to work for God, not yourself. Accept His love and His

plan for proper rest for you. Learn to say "No" to others at least once a day.

Psalms 107:8-9 Let them give thanks to the Lord for His unfailing love and His wonderful deeds for men, for He satisfies the thirsty and fills the hungry with good things.

5. Perhaps your burnout has no relation to your work. You are simply in a rut and feel like you are in a "rat race". You go from activity to activity, or your health struggles and you live with pain that is adversely affecting you. You seem to have lost focus. You have lost tract of the fact that it is God who preserves your life, not you.

Psalm 138:7 Though I walk in the middle of trouble, You preserve my life.

Psalm 143:11 For Your name's sake, O Lord, preserve my life; in Your righteousness, bring me out of trouble.

Memory verse for Burnout:

Psalm 4:8 I will lie down and *sleep in* peace, for You alone, O Lord, make me dwell in safety.

15 Worry (Anxiety)

"We can easily manage if we will only take each day, the burden appointed to it. But the load will be too heavy for us if we carry yesterday's burden over again today, and then add the burden of the morrow before we are required to bear it."

- John Newton (1725-1807), author of "Amazing Grace"

Definition: a state of uncertainty over actual or potential problems, allowing one's mind to dwell on the difficulty or troubles.

Worry is the most common non-medical problem that I see in clinical practice. I estimate that it is 5-10 times more common than depression. Depression steps into the picture when people develop chronic anxiety states. At times, my patients will exhibit a "mixed bag" of anxiety and depression simultaneously. Virtually all the problems presented in this book can bring worry to the surface. In the office, there are some scoring systems that are valuable in evaluating anxiety. The *Hamilton Anxiety Rating Scale* (HAM-A; 1959) is helpful in the initial evaluation of anxiety and for follow-up scoring. It classifies the symptoms *and* severity. Here is the survey:

Symptoms: 0- absent; 1- mild; 2- moderate; 3- severe; 4- incapacitating

Anxious Mood- worries or anticipates worst	0-4
Tension- startles, cries, restless, trembling	0-4
Fears- dark, stranger, being alone, animals	0-4
Insomnia- falling/staying asleep; nightmares	0-4
Intellectual- poor concentration; poor memory	0-4
Depressed mood- decreased interest	0-4
Somatic (muscular) complaints- aches	0-4
Sensory complaints- tinnitus; blurry vision	0-4
Cardiovascular- fast heartrate, chest pain	0-4
Respiratory- SOB, choking	0-4
Gastrointestinal- N/V, constipation	0-4
Genitourinary- ED, urinary frequency	0-4
Autonomic- dry mouth, flushing, sweating	0-4
Behavior- fidgets, tremor, paces	0-4

Score: < 17- mild; 18-24- mild to moderate; 25-30- moderate to severe

---

According to data from the National Institute of Mental Health, some 38% of girls ages 13 through 17, and 26% of boys, have an anxiety disorder. On college campuses, anxiety is running well ahead of depression as the most common mental health concern, according to a 2016 national study of more than 150,000 students by the Center for Collegiate Mental Health at Pennsylvania State University. Meanwhile, the number of web searches involving the term "worry" has nearly doubled over the last five years, according to Google Trends. The trendline for "depression" was relatively flat. - *Alex Williams, "Prozac Nation Is Now the United States of Xanax," New York Times (6-10-17)*

Historians will probably call our era "the age of worry." Though we have it easier than our forefathers, we have more uneasiness. Billy Graham, the great Christian evangelist, agrees that inwardly we are more anxious. "Callused hands were the badge of the pioneers and ancestors, but a furrowed brow is the insignia of modern men and women," Billy was quoted as saying.

Everyone has anxiety now and then. You might get nervous before a big test in school, when you meet with the tax auditor, go the dentist, or just before you are in a big performance. When I was growing up, I frequently got the "butterflies in my stomach" before an important baseball game in which I was pitching, or during a conference swim meet if I was part of the last freestyle

It's normal to get nervous before a race

relay. But there's a difference between getting jittery and letting it boil over to worry. If worry begins to hold your attention too much and prevent you from functioning normally, then it is a problem. Worrying causes excessive inward contemplation and an inability to relax.

People with mild or moderate perfectionistic tendencies are especially prone to worry. For those who are high performers and who have an element of compulsivity in their personality, they might be more challenged to worry than others. When they are in control and the correct results happen in a situation, all is well. However, when there is an uncontrollable event that can't be fixed, perfectionists can get more tense. If they are unable to "fix things" quickly, they are more likely to obsess on a solution. This causes anxiety.

External factors (outside our control) *most commonly* cause worry. These include:

- Work problems- new project, new boss, new rules
- School problems- new teacher, hard subject
- Money problems- paying off debt, new bills to pay
- Death of a family member, friend, or pet
- New medical illness- heart attack, stroke, low blood sugar
- Medication side effects- such as blood pressure meds
- Use of recreational drugs/addiction- caffeine, nicotine
- Loss of control- a tornado whips through your neighborhood
- Insecurity- you get in a car accident and your car is "totaled"
- Major changes in life (such as moving to a new location)
- Conflicts in any meaningful relationship; husband/wife
- Social interaction with strangers
- Fears of any kind; such a fear of flying

Look at these statistics on worry:

- A very high percent of what we worry about never comes to pass.
- 30% of what we worry about happened in the past and can't be changed.
- 10% of what we worry about relates to health. (Researchers have proven that worry makes your health worse not better)
- 8% of worry is legitimate, but even then, worry won't change the conclusion!

Researcher Lucas LaFreniere, Ph.D. said, "This is what breaks my heart about worry. It makes you miserable in the present moment to try and prevent misery in the future. For chronic worriers, this process leads them to be continually distressed all their lives in order to avoid later events that never happen. Worry sucks the joy out of the 'here and now.'" In his study on worry, participants were asked to record their worries and how they caused distress and interfered with their lives. Each night at 10 pm, they reported how much time they spent thinking on each specific worry throughout the day. Then, 20 days after that period, they reviewed each entry and reported whether any of the worries had become true. The good news is the study found that in his survey of worrisome people, 91.4 percent of their worries never actually happened. Worrying caused only more misery and did nothing to help the worriers handle whatever they had been worrying about. This is mainly because the hotly anticipated events never transpired. -*Sarah Sloat, "Researchers Prove That What You're Worried About Isn't Likely to Come True" Inverse (8-4-19)*

See how *internal* worry affects us? We know that worry doesn't help us in any way, but we still do it. Much of what we worry about is an exaggerated emotion in response to something that never happens. For example, you're trying to sleep, and it's well after bedtime. You're tossing and turning and unable to get comfortable. You notice you're replaying the same scenario in your head. Some vision of tomorrow, of what might happen, how a hope could be dashed. If you've had this experience, you're far from alone. Insomnia is a symptom of worry.

Frequently, my patients will go to physical therapy sessions after their orthopedic surgery knowing that they will experience a lot of pain. They are often tense about the get-together. The therapist stretches the affected extremity and holds it in positions that it hasn't been for quite a while. After holding each painful position for a minute or so, the therapist will say, "Okay, you can hang loose." The patients will tell me later, "I think I heard that at least 25 times in each therapy session: 'Okay, you can hang loose, take a break.'

I think these words can apply to the rest of our lives as well. We can relax in God's goodness and faithfulness instead of worrying. When Jesus neared his death, he knew his disciples would need help because of their worries and fears being without him. To encourage them, Jesus said he would send them the Holy Spirit to remind them of what he had taught them (read **John 14:26**). "Peace I leave with you; my peace I give you. Do not let your hearts be troubled and do not be afraid" (read **John 14:27**). There are plenty of things we can be upset or uneasy about in daily living. From an unpleasant neighbor to bad weather to global terrorism. But we can learn to trust God and remember that his Spirit lives in us to give us a peace that surpasses all understanding. As we derive strength from him, we can hear him say, "Okay, you can hang loose."

There is a key principle taught about worry in the story of Mike Bechtle's lawn. "In some parts of my lawn, the grass is thick and green. In other areas, it's sparse and dry. There are even a few places where the grass is missing entirely. When I mow the lawn, I notice that where the grass is healthy, there are no weeds. Where the lawn is sparse, there are a few. Where there is no grass, the weeds flourish. Every time I notice the weedy spots, I think, I really need to pull those things. So I do, but within a few weeks they're back - and I'm pulling them again. One day it hit me: I do not have to pull weeds where the grass is thick. Instead of spending all my time pulling weeds, maybe I [need] to invest time making the grass as healthy as possible. The more grass I had the fewer weeds I would have to pull. The same applies to worry. Worry is like the weeds. God's peace is the grass. Instead of just focusing on eliminating my worries, I need to cultivate God's peace." *-Mike Bechtle, in Discipleship magazine; quoted in the October 21, 2008.*

Prescription for Worry: God wants you to know you can find peace of mind in Him alone, the author of a peace that surpasses all understanding. Learn to GO TO GOD FIRST with all your worries and cares.

1. Who can you trust for all your cares in life? No human can provide these. God can be trusted in every detail.

    Psalms 40:3b-4a Many will see and fear (have an awe for) and put their trust in the Lord. Blessed is the person who makes the Lord his trust.

2. Worrying about the future hampers your efforts for today. Your future is in God's hands. He will help direct you on your path.

    Psalm 143:8 Let the morning bring me word of Your unfailing love, for I have put my trust in You. Show me the way I should go, for to You I lift up my soul.

3. Worrying is more harmful to your health than helpful regarding the situation you are worried about. Beware. God will continue to preserve your life.

Psalm 119:50 My comfort in my suffering is this; Your promises preserve my life.

Psalm 94:19 When anxiety was great within me, Your consolation brought joy to my soul.

4. God does not ignore those who are dependent on Him. Learn to depend on Him and not the circumstances in your life that you are worried about.

    Psalms 66:18-19 If I had cherished sin in my heart, the Lord would not have listened; but God has surely listened and heard my voice in prayer.

5. Worry shows a lack of faith in God. Seek to increase your faith.

    Psalm 40:16 But may all who seek You rejoice and be glad in You; may those who love Your salvation always say, "The Lord be exalted!"

6. Live one day at a time with God guiding you. Don't look too far ahead or behind you.

    Psalm 67:4 May the nations be glad and sing for joy, for You (God) rule the peoples justly and guide the nations of the earth.

7. Worry turns your focus off God and only lead to evil.

    Psalm 37:8b Do not fret—it leads only to evil.

Memory verse for Worry:

Psalm 91:2 I will say of the Lord, "He is my refuge and my fortress, my God, in whom I trust."

16	# Moral Failure

"The Bible will keep you from sin, or sin will keep you from the Bible."

-Dwight L. Moody, Christian evangelist and publisher

<u>Definition</u>: an immoral act considered to be a violation against someone else or God's moral law(s); a deliberate rebellion by choosing wrong against God's principles. God calls moral failure *sin*.

All of us can admit that we fall short morally because none of us are perfect. The path we are on in our lives *IS ABOUT* decisions that we make day to day. Often, these determinations are

of a small consequence. But sometimes we make a wrong decision that can adversely affect our lives going into the future. Think about the warnings that your parents probably gave to you in high school. "Be careful what friends you pick and hang out with," they said. For example, bad influences coupled with peer pressure might lead to casual smoking, then vaping, then marijuana, then other drugs of abuse like heroin, methamphetamine, or cocaine. The addict says, "I shouldn't have started that first puff on the cigarette."

People magazine once undertook a survey of its readers on 'sin'. The results were published as a "Sindex," with each sin rated by a sin coefficient. The outcome was both amusing and instructive. Sins like murder, child abuse, and spying against one's country were rated the worst sins in ascending order, with smoking, swearing, and illegal videotaping far down the list. Parking in a handicapped spot was rated surprising high, whereas unmarried live-togethers got off lightly. Cutting in front of someone in line was deemed worse than divorce or capital punishment. Predictably, corporate sin was not mentioned at all. The survey concluded, "Overall, readers said they commit about 4.64 sins a month. (that's all?)" People want to categorize sin. They want to say that some sins are much worse than others. Parking in a handicapped spot is high, but living together before marriage is low? Many would say that living together before marriage is not a sin. "Everybody is doing it" so it must be 'OK'. Cutting in front of someone in line is worse than capital punishment? Who determines the severity of sin?

Many believe moral failure or *sin* is an archaic term that is not relevant in our world. Many do not believe in the existence of God, the Creator of the Universe, or his moral laws. Sin is not something that people want to talk about. It's also a term that they don't want to apply to themselves. The idea of guilt from sin is 'out of date' and unhealthy. The heinous serial killer or the rapist may be evil and a sinner, but not them. ISIS terrorists may be evil but not them.

Outrageous acts of immorality are explained by "environmental pressures". "It's not really the Chicago gang member's fault they kill each other" (there are over 500 murders/year in Chicago, and many are related to gang violence). They are dysfunctional because of lack of proper parenting and guidance. "Someone else is to blame." In the photo on the left is Dwayne Wade, former NBA basketball star, speaking out on gun violence.

Or our culture says abortion isn't murder of a living fetus; it's ultimately the "choice of the mother," and it's nobody else's business.

Politicians, educators, sociologists and others try to "fix" our society from its' waywardness, but they can't do it. Their premise is that mankind is "basically good" and that with the right circumstances, people will make the right decisions. How incorrect that this premise is.

In the last 40 years, our culture is not improving in moral choices. Why? Because our culture can't fix men and women who have brokenness in their hearts. We inherit corruption-prone in action, thought, emotion, and will from when we are born. We proudly think our way is the right way. Any deviation from that is wrong, and we disagree. Underneath it all, we are resentful towards those who disagree with us.

We sin by thinking evil, speaking evil, acting evil, and omitting good. To say that we have a "bent towards do wrong" from birth? To say that there is a desire in us to rebel against the morality of God's rules even as a child? That will raise some eyebrows, but I can tell you my friend, the truth is the truth. I did not have to teach my two y/o child how to be rebellious from the rules.

What is our society's standard today for determining what is evil? At one time, it was the Bible. In the last generation, that is changing. We are now sliding down the slippery slope of sin and changing our moral values, not paying attention to absolute authority. In fact, everybody's right, and political correctness is the religion of our time.

Being politically correct even hits the Christian church. Four congregation members with concerned faces met in their pastor's office. With earnest and imploring eyes, they presented him with a clipboard filled with sheets of signatures. "This petition," said the spokesperson of the group, "requests changing the term 'sinner' to 'person who is morally challenged.'" - *from an original cartoon by Dan Pegoda, The Best Cartoons from Leadership Journal.*

Because God loved us, he gave us a set of guidelines for how we should live found in the book of Exodus. In the Sermon on the Mount in the Gospel of **Matthew 5-7**, Jesus gave us an internal standard to live by. God knew that we would tend towards a defiant attitude and rebel against him. He knew that we would tend toward ungratefulness and think that everything we have is not because of him. Despite this, he chose to love us. All the food the sinner eats, the air they breathe, the joys they experience, are all gifts from God. The sinner who does not know God embraces all gifts not knowing that God is in control of all. Even when we are armed with the blueprint of the Bible for right living, we continue to screw up. Why? Because we are drawn towards sin.

God knew that we would tend towards wandering from him, and:

1) Put other gods before him- striving for material wealth and power
2) Build monuments to ourselves and put our names on buildings, or erect idols of worship
3) Cheapen his name by using it as a replacement for cuss words
4) Use the day of rest once a week not to worship him, but to lounge around and go boating, ice fishing, or watch football games
5) Not be respectful of our parents, but mock them for doing a lousy job
6) Kill people not only physically, but also in our hearts through unresolved anger
7) Commit adultery and defile sex through anything but a normal heterogeneous marriage relationship
8) Steal not only money but also other people's ideas; all to improve ourselves in a false way
9) Lie by exaggeration, embellishment, or in a disguised manner to "save face" or make ourselves look better than we are
10) Be envious and jealous of everything that your neighbor has, breeding resentment into the future and preventing a good relationship with them

That is why God gave us the Ten Commandments in **Exodus 20:3-17.** By giving us these laws, he was telling us, "If you keep these set of guidelines or rules, it will free you from even more *dysfunction* in your life"

Hypocrisy is at the center of many of our ongoing sins. Hypocrisy is when our conscience knows what is wrong, but we disobey and do it anyway, or we know what is right, but we do not follow through. Let us give some examples:

- You talk about saving the environment but then you litter by disposing your beer bottles and soda cans off the side of boat while fishing "because nobody will see the bottles and cans on the bottom of the lake"
- As a 19 y/o teenager, you warn everyone about the dangers of texting while driving and then you cross the center line while texting and cause a head-on car crash, killing the other driver
- You complain about the difficulties at work and then you go on your Facebook page for hours when your boss is away on vacation
- You gossip about a good friend and you know it is wrong, but you do it anyway
- You know that no children should go hungry, but you continue to eat like a glutton in the millions of restaurants in our country, where 22-33 billion pounds/year of food waste occurs
- You know that it is important to tell the truth, but then when somebody tells you the truth that you do not want to accept, you close your ears

- You tell your teenage son not to speed when he gets his new driver's license, but with him in the back seat watching, you proceed to go 50 MPH in a 35 MPH because you are late for a choir rehearsal
- You teach your kids not to steal, and then you cheat on your income taxes and the government catches you
- You complain about government bureaucracy, and then you refuse to vote at the next election
- You are an avid advocate of a "Saving the Whales" campaign, and then you proceed to have an abortion. Looks like you care more about whales than a human life.

The above list can go on and on with countless examples of not only how often we sin but also that we need a prescription for our rebellious ways. We should face the facts: we all tend towards hypocrisy. We *choose* to make mistake sometimes that are nonsensical and against godly principles. Do you surprise yourself with your inability to follow upright rules of thought and conduct? Likely.

In his book *The Sins We Love*, Randy Rowland outlines the seven sins or moral failures that entrap people. #1- PRIDE; I am proud of being proud and what I accomplish #2- ENVY- I want what I haven't got #3- ANGER- I'm mad that you did something wrong #4- SLOTH- I'm taking care of me right now #5 GREED- It's mine, mine, mine #6- GLUTTONY- I want it all and I want it now and #7- LUST- it's ok to look, isn't it? All these sins are readily apparent in us as well as our society. Do an inventory in your own life.

Erwin Lutzer, Pastor Emeritus of Moody Bible Church in Chicago (in  photo on left), tells a story about the temptation towards pride, even in a "good work" that he performed. He was out making a call on a country highway and came upon a little old lady stopped in her car on the side of the road. Dutifully, he stopped to help her as there was nothing around for miles. "I ran out of gas and don't have a cellphone," she told him. He told her that he would drive to the nearest gas station and get some gas and bring it back to help her. "That would be so nice, thank you!" He obediently drove and picked up a few gallons of gas at a station five miles away and brought it back to the lady to finish his mission. Up to this point, you could say this was just a good deed done by a Pastor of a large evangelical church. Then Pastor Lutzer goes on, "As I was pouring the gas into the lady's gas tank, all of the sudden I thought, "Wouldn't it be nice if people in my congregation could see me doing this?"" Haha! All the sudden- that's how Satan plays with your mind. A prime example of how pride rears its ugly head. How pride wants to take credit. How pride wants its' ego "built up". Be careful in your good works that you don't sabotage them for Satan. Pride should not be a motivator for good works, but it often is.

In his book *How to Say No to a Stubborn Habit* (1982), Lutzer says: "Sinful habits begin innocently enough, but if we do not master them, they will surely master us. Here is the cycle: enjoy a forbidden pleasure, feel guilty, determine never to do it again, take pride in brief moments of self-control, then fail once more." Pride can be a nasty habit.

Self-worship (putting yourself first in relationships) is at the heart of greed, lust, selfishness, all are forms of self-worship … Here is a typical example: in Phnom Penh, Cambodia, a 14 y/o girl was sold to a brothel for sex trafficking by her father. As a victim of her father's self-worship, she was reduced to a solution for a desire or need that he had. She was the sacrifice to his self-worship. Every time she was raped for pay, the man raping her used her to gratify his perverted sexual desires in an act of self-worship. The brothel owners who commoditize her flesh were worshiping self as they daily exchanged her pain for their profit. Sex trafficking is a worldwide problem that exemplifies SELF.

While this was most vivid in the red-light districts of Cambodia, the reality is that self-worship is at the heart of nearly every decision that we make today. That same self-worship is at the heart of our decisions to go to porn sites and pay for the flesh of the downtrodden and oppressed, our decisions to purchase products manufactured by known violators of child labor laws, and our decisions to consume foods and beverages that come from people who receive little or nothing for their labor. In the end, we are all Phnom Penh. We are all a part of the nightmare, and we are all unfit for the dream of God. - *R. York Moore, Making All Things New (IVP Books, 2013)*

Just like there are prescriptions found in the Psalms for anger, depression, burnout, worry, post-traumatic stress, sickness, fears, suffering, loneliness, and grief, there are godly prescriptions for our moral failures and sin. In order to understand the cure, it is of utmost importance to start from the beginning….to review how the problem of sin started and how only God *has the cure*.

For reasons known only to God, he decided to populate earth (after he created it) with humans created in his image who would choose to worship him by obeying his will. He created us to have a superior mind above any other living creature. He breathed into man his Spirit and gave him a soul to live forever. By design, humans would procreate more humans like themselves enabling them to obey or disobey God as they chose. They would have the ability to pass on these traits to hundreds of future generations.

Sin was injected into humanity with the help of Satan (Lucifer), who aided Adam and Eve in disobeying God by eating from the forbidden tree (read **Genesis 3**). God had told Adam and Eve not to eat the forbidden trees' fruit, but they did it anyway. Why God placed mankind on this earth- where a fallen Satan had access to people's minds and will- we are not told. God simply chose to create a world that was capable, because of free will, of rebelling against Him. He did not want to create a bunch of zombies. Sin has plagued mankind since. Men and women choose to responsibly disobey God today, just like yesterday. In every generation, people must choose whom they will serve; God,

Satan, some other god, or themselves. Many choose not to believe that God exists, and that he did not create the universe.

From the beginning, God chose to work especially in a group of people  on earth called the Israelites. He chose to have his history recorded in the Bible, made up of the Old and New Testament. Jehovah God (Yahweh), the God of Christians today, makes it crystal clear in the Bible that THERE IS NO GOD except him. He is the Creator of all things ever made, from the smallest electron to the entire universe and beyond. He is before all things and after all things. Yahweh is the name of the one, true God meaning "I AM," represented in Hebrew by the tetragrammaton ("four letters") יהוה (Yod Heh Vav Heh), which was transliterated into Roman script as Y H W H. Because it was considered blasphemous to utter the name of God, the name was only written and never spoken, which resulted in the original pronunciation becoming lost.

There are six facts the name Yahweh, "I AM," says about God:

1. God never had a beginning. Every child asks, "Who made God?" And every wise parent says, "Nobody made God. God simply is. And always was. No beginning and no end."
2. God is absolute reality. There is no reality before him. There is no reality outside of him unless he wills it and makes it. He is all that was eternally. No space, no universe, no emptiness. Only God.
3. God is utterly independent. He depends on nothing to bring him into being or support him or counsel him or make him what he is.
4. Everything that is not God depends totally on God. The entire universe is utterly secondary. It came into being by God and stays in being moment by moment on God's decision to keep it in being.
5. God is constant. He is the same yesterday, today, and forever. He cannot be improved. He is not becoming anything. He is who he is.
6. God is the absolute standard of truth and goodness and beauty. There is no lawbook to which he looks to know what is right. No almanac to establish facts. No guild to determine what is excellent or beautiful. He himself is the standard of what is right and what is true.

In **Genesis 3:16-3:19**, God establishes that there are *consequences of disobedience* to him. It's called punishment. A law (rule) was established by him, and it was broken. This would become a universal moral absolute and would be a warning for all future generations of humans for the rest of time. This principle is key. God is a God of justice. Laws are a good thing. They establish boundaries for mankind. What good is a law, if there is no authority over the lawbreaker or punishment for the law? God is that authority.

Let us look at some examples of usurping God's authority, the ultimate sin of people. In the second book of the Old Testament, God said to the Hebrew leader Moses (1304-1237 B.C.), "Say this to my chosen people of Israel, 'The LORD, the God of your fathers, the God of Abraham, the God of Isaac, and the

God of Jacob, has sent me to you.' This is My name forever, and thus I am to be remembered throughout all generations." (**Exodus 3)** God made his supremacy known to the people of the earth, but especially the Israelites. One of the best

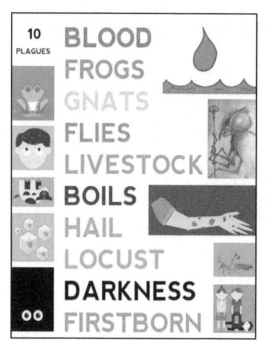

examples was when he showed the prominent leader-pharaoh of pagan country Egypt who was really in control; that he alone was the God of the universe. At the time of Moses, the Israelites had been enslaved in Egypt for hundreds of years and at that time had lost faith in the God of their forefathers. They believed he existed, but they doubted that He could, or would, break the yoke of their bondage. The Egyptians, like many pagan cultures, worshiped a wide variety of nature-gods and attributed to their powers to the natural phenomena they saw in the world around them. Like we can, they worshipped the created rather than the Creator. By allowing the ten plagues for punishment of the Egyptians, God dismantled their belief systems one by one. He mightily revealed his power over all the Egyptian man-made gods.

God used the Hebrew leaders Moses and Aaron as his ambassadors in delivering these mighty plagues on the Egyptians.

The following Egyptian gods correlate with the ten plagues, one through ten:

Khnum, Apis, Isis- gods of the Nile River- plague of Egypt's water system- turned to blood

Heqet- god of fertility- plague of frogs

Khepri- god of insects- plague of gnats, flies, and locust

Set- god of the desert- plague of gnats

Uatchit- god of flies- plague of the flies Hathor and Apis- gods of cattle- plague of the livestock

Sekhmet, Sunu - gods of good health and disease- plague of boils

Nut- god of the sky- plague of hail

Osiris- crop fertility god- plague of hail, locusts

Set- god of storms- plague of hail

Re- god of the sun- plague of darkness

Isis- god of child protection- plague of death of the firstborn

Through these plagues, God exhibited his control over the universe in these ways:

His control over weather/nature- plague of hail, water system into blood

His control over life- plague of death of the firstborn

His control over animals and living creatures- plague of the frogs, gnats, flies, locusts, livestock

His control over microscopic, unseen germs- plague of boils

His control over astronomy- plague of darkness

From the Bible, we know that God despises moral failure/sin but loves the person committing the sin. Sinful behavior is an affront to God's character- his holiness and his laws. God cannot just look the other way and pretend evil does not exist. In the end, he must punish sin.

King David, the author of most the Psalms, knew plenty about moral failure. The story of his sexual sin with Bathsheba in **2 Samuel 11** should be a sober warning for us. He broke a minimum of the last five of the Ten Commandments (see **Exodus 20:13-17**) in this life story alone.

#6: "Do not kill..." David had Bathsheba's husband killed so he could have her to himself. Uriah was killed in battle when he was put in the front lines. It was the arrows of others that David used to kill Uriah.

#7: "Do not commit adultery..." this was the clearest of all David's law breaking. He lusted after the gorgeous and naked Bathsheba

#8: "Do not steal..." David stole the wife of his neighbor and trusted friend Uriah as the prophet Nathan later pointed out.

#9: "Do not lie..." David's false response was a lie when the messenger came with the ghastly news of Uriah's death; and even more, every day David living in sin was a lie that he deceptively covered up.

#10: "Do not covet..." David broke this law as he coveted his neighbors' wife that he would steal her and kill her husband to lie in sexual sin with her.

Many think that David lived a "charmed" life, and that God showed favor on him. I can tell you it was *not* because of his many sins! There are consequences of sin in our lives, and King David and his family paid for them:

Michal- his first wife and Saul's daughter, was childless and could not get pregnant, which was a travesty in those times. David gave her 5 nephews to the Gibeonites to be killed because of Saul's sins. Wow!

Ahinoam- his wife, had Amnon, David's firstborn. Amnon raped Tamar, his half-sister, and was later killed by Absalom for revenge. Wow!

Maacah- his wife, had Absalom, David's 3rd son, and Tamar, David's only daughter named. He rebelled against his father David.

Haggith- his wife, had Adonijah, David's 4th son. He was never disciplined. He set himself up as king before David's death. Solomon later had him executed. Wow again!

Bathsheba- had an unnamed son with David who died in infancy. Later had Solomon (who was David and Bathsheba's 4th son together), who was the next king of Israel.

Throughout history, it is readily apparent that no human is exempt from sin and moral failure. Everyone is under this curse. To be cured from the curse, we must understand our hearts, and that our hearts bend toward sin. We must understand that sin cannot be cured from a human perspective. Sin must always be dealt with. It is why things are the way they are. It is why there are constant wars, factions, bickering, conflicts, crime, and rebellion from what is right. Nationally, locally, and personally. Once we comprehend that sin has a strong "hold on us", we will appreciate the need for a cure from a deceitful heart.

In the fullness of time, God showed his love for the people on earth by sending his only son Jesus to live with us as a human that whosoever would believe in Jesus and what he did on the cross would never perish but have eternal life. Jesus Christ, who is God, lived for 33 years as the only sinless person who ever walked the face of the earth. He took on the full weight of sin's guilt on himself and bore the punishment for it. He died on a cross in a terrible death of crucifixion as a substitute for sinners. Those who believe and trust in the mighty work of Jesus receive forgiveness and mercy because he has already paid the price for our moral failures, past, present, and future. The cross represents both the wrath of God on sin and the grace shown to the sinner. God will forever embrace the sinner who comes to him in humble repentance and asks in faith for forgiveness.

King David was a mighty sinner. And so are we. We all fall short of God's laws and have moral failures. None are perfect. However, David was also called a "man after God's heart (read **1 Samuel 13:14**). Is that puzzling to you? Despite David's sexual exploits, about 1,000 years later, the incarnate God chose to live on the earth through King David's lineage. In the Gospel of Matthew, Jesus is called the son of King David, indicating his royal origin, and the Son of Abraham, indicating that he was an Israelite. Son means descendant, calling to mind the promises God made to David and to Abraham in the Old Testament. God chose to love David despite his sin and he does the same for you.

The following words describe the *heart of King David* as seen in the Psalms. He was:

Humble - Lowborn men are but a breath, the highborn are but a lie; if weighed on a balance, they are nothing; together they are only a breath. **Psalm 62:9**
Trusting - The Lord is my light and my salvation—whom will I fear? The Lord is the stronghold of my life—of whom shall I be afraid? **Psalm 27:1**
Loving - I love you, O Lord, my strength. **Psalm 18:1**
Devoted -You have filled my heart with greater joy than when their grain and new wine abound. **Psalm 4:7**
Faithful- Surely goodness and love will follow me all the days of my life, and I will dwell in the house of the Lord forever. **Psalm 23:6**
Obedient - Give me understanding, and I will keep your law and obey it with all my heart. **Psalm 119:34**

<u>Repentant</u> -For the sake of your name, O Lord, forgive my iniquity, though it is great. **Psalm 25:11**

Prescription for Moral Failure: God knows that you are far from perfect. He knows that at times you *will* fail in moral conduct. Like David, you should reach out to Him with your failures and repent of your sins. Learn to GO TO GOD FIRST with your moral bankruptcy and He will save you.

1. First things first. Admit that you have moral failures, you are accountable, and that you need forgiveness, and that God is stronger than your sin. Talk about them to God specifically and regularly.

   Psalm 51:1-2 Have mercy on me, O God, according to Your unfailing love; according to Your great compassion blot out my transgressions. Wash away all my iniquity and cleanse me from my sin.

2. God hears your prayers all times of the day and wants to preserve your moral health. Steady progress is possible. You must believe that you can be delivered. The answers to your prayers are related to your attitude of repentance.

   Psalms 55:16-18 But I call to God, and the Lord saves me. Evening, morning, and noon I cry out in distress, and He hears my voice. He ransoms me unharmed from the battle wages against me, even though many oppose me.

3. When you feel afflicted in your sins, go to God and He will give you mercy. Mercy is forgiveness when you deserve punishment. He wants your attitudes and actions to be whole again.

   Psalms 25:16-18 Turn to me and be gracious to me, for I am lonely and afflicted. The troubles of my heart have multiplied; free me from my anguish. Look upon my affliction and my distress and take away all my sins.

4. God's desire is to save you forever so that you can be in fellowship with Him in heaven eternally. Hell (eternal separation from God) need not have dominion over you.

   Psalms 40:3b-4a Many will see and fear (have an awe for) and put their trust in the Lord. Blessed is the person who makes the Lord his trust.

<u>Memory verse for Moral Failure</u>:

   Psalm 71:3 Be my Rock of refuge, to which I can always go; give the command to save me, for You are my Rock and my Fortress.

17 Consequences of Life's Stressors

In previous centuries of cultures and civilizations thousands of years ago, infections were the most common causes of disease. People were fortunate to live into their sixties. Without vaccines, infant and child deaths were sky high because of contagious diseases which did awful things to their victims. A perfect example of this was a bacterium called Hemophilus influenza. It caused 35,000 cases/year in the U.S. of infant bacterial meningitis at its' peak. Along the way, it spawned not only cranial nerve palsies like hearing loss, but also death. Since the H. flu vaccine (called 'Hib') came out in the 1980s, the disease has been pretty much eradicated. Similarly, vaccines have wiped out diseases like smallpox, measles, diphtheria, polio, tetanus, and many others.

Today, in the industrialized nations of the world, other ailments are contributing significantly to morbidity and mortality, including heart disease, stroke, accidents, and cancer. Of course, these diseases can be curtailed but will never go away. In addition to these physical illnesses, mental stressors (and difficulties brought on by one's response to stressors) have become more widely commonplace. Stressors 'response' and the damage they impart have become the number one reason why people visit healthcare providers.

No question that addiction, anger, boredom, change, depression, discouragement, fear, guilt, loneliness, insecurity, pain, sickness, burnout, worry, and moral failure add more pressures to our lives than we would like. These stressors lead to emotional tension. Tension then has snowball effects and negatively affects our bodies with proven increased levels of adrenaline and cortisone. Normally, these hormones only rise in the "fight or flight" response of the human body. However, when stressors are invading our lives daily, we can bet on more and more hormonal imbalance. Higher hormone levels which are not healthy for prolonged periods of time have some damaging effect on our bodies. This is just one example of how our bodies can get "out of sync" when hormone levels explode to the upside.

Bodily effects of psychological stresses can produce these physical problems:

Disorders of the Digestive system: ulcers of the stomach, flare up of inflammatory bowel disease like ulcerative colitis, and spastic colon. Other problems include poor appetite and hiccups. Indeed, there ARE nerves in the bowel from the esophagus to the rectum.

Disorders of the Circulatory system: Blood pressure can elevate. Other disorders include fast heart rate (Paroxysmal atrial tachycardia), irregular pulses (atrial fibrillation), migraine headaches, and angina (a worsening blockage).

Disorders of the Genito-Urinary system: menstrual cycle irregularity, painful sex, frequent urination, and impotence.

101

Disorders of the Nervous system: seizures, neuroses (OCD, anxiety), hyperventilation.

Disorders of the Allergic/Pulmonary system: hives, itching, asthma attacks.

Disorders of the Muscle-joint system: fibromyalgia, backpain, muscle tension anywhere

Disorders of the Dermatology system: scratching, picking, neurodermatitis, Raynaud's or capillary spasm of the skin (making it change purple or white, and get cold)

Disorders of the nutritional system: anorexia nervosa, morbid obesity, addictions.

This list is the short version; there are many other body problems directly related to stress.

The last thing you want in your life is to fight the uphill battle against stress by yourself. Not only can you be mentally paralyzed and imprisoned mentally, but your body can pay for it also. Do yourself a huge favor if you have not yet. Begin *now* to be intentional in your response to stress. That means daily. Learn to **Go to God First** with all your burdens. He is *by far* the best prescription for your daily needs.

18 Memories

"Let your memory be your travel bag."

-Aleksandr Solzhenitsyn,
famous Russian novelist

Your memories are housed in your brain. Your brain contains 100 billion cells, and each neuron can form tens of thousands of connections with other neurons. An important function of the brain is to sort out what you should remember and not remember. God designed the brain so that only some memories last. Memories *are* your life, so to speak, and mold you. Memories are believed to go from short-to long-term memory by reinforcement. Initially, the synapses involved in a memory trace are very weak. However, with repetition or a link to strong emotions, the connections become stronger and stronger.

Your failure to remember where you left your car keys somewhere isn't necessarily a sign of senility. It shows your brain is working well, sorting out things that really matter in life. Your inability to remember things like where you have left things can be annoying. Yet if you understand how your brain works--you can gain a whole new appreciation for this marvel.

You may mistakenly believe that the brain stores all the information it encounters, but you just cannot always access it. In fact, you forget many things, which appear to be gone forever. And that is a good thing.

Consider what happens if you remember everything. One psychology patient could remember lists of hundreds of random words without even trying, but this posed a problem. He had trouble forgetting anything. Even worse, he had difficulty distinguishing between useful and useless information. His brain was overloaded.

God created your brain to process a steady stream of information—thousands of bits pour into your brain every few seconds from all your five senses. As you monitor the world, your brain must discard useless details and latch onto anything of short-term or long-term value.

When memories are sweet and pleasant, there is nothing like reminiscing through your travel bag, as Solzhenitsyn says in the initial quote of this chapter. It's soothing to think back about wonderful people you have met in the past, beautiful landscapes you have experienced, and jobs you have accomplished. These snapshots in your memories fill you with joy.

Think attentively about your life. There are multitude of memories that you have forgotten and can be pulled out of your computer of a brain *only if* reminded about specifically. Let us face it, many experiences in life are not worth remembering. Many of your days are filled with monotony, but interspersed sporadically are domineering memories, good or bad.

For example, many of my fondest memories feel like they happened yesterday. The day I received the gift of Christian faith at age 13 in the narthex at Northwest Covenant Church in Mt. Prospect, Illinois with Pastor Engseth interceding with me. The day I was accepted to medical school was 4 PM,

Friday, December 4th, 1976. I still remember where I opened the letter in the parking lot at Northwestern University, the temperature in the air, how I felt when I saw the typing saying that I was accepted, and the fact that it was lightly snowing. Another is of my wedding day on a gorgeous fall day-- October 15th, 1988. I remember all the wonderful details—the beauty of my wife Janet, the joy of our families, the reception, etc. Memories are like that. They allow you to re-live special times in your life.

The word 'reminisce' invokes 'warmth and fuzzies'. Reminisce magazine captivates your good memories. Each issue focuses on a particular year in history, let us say 1983. It allows you to 'go back in time' and remember what it was like then-the cost of a gallon of gas, the types of cars we drove, the different clothes that we wore, and how we wore our hair! It can be fun to reminisce about old times.

However, your memories are a two-edged sword. It has been said that people have an annoying habit of remembering things that they should not remember. This 'habit' is at the center of many mental health problems like post-traumatic stress disorder, phobias, anger, depression, and worry.

You may be emotionally wounded in your memories; maybe from a childhood trauma or horrendous accident you were in when friends were killed but you were not (such as a motor vehicle accident). You are ripe for PTSD and other mental dysfunctions. Insomnia (an inability to sleep) can 'step in' and tell you (through your memories) that you are going stay awake and review dumb things you did and mean things someone said to you. You then re-live regrets you have, mistakes you have made, and distresses you have known.

Real life can be ripped apart by recurrent and agonizing memories of past injuries. The negative memories are a main problem in PTSD patients-- and there is a science behind this. In PTSD patients, parts of the brain involved in emotional processing appear different in brain scans. One important part of the brain responsible for memory and emotions is known as the *hippocampus*. In people with PTSD, the hippocampus appears smaller in size. It is thought

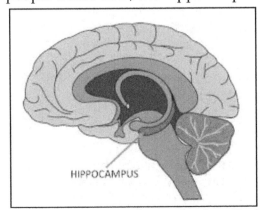

that changes in this part of the brain may be related to fear and anxiety, memory problems and flashbacks. A malfunctioning hippocampus may prevent flashbacks and nightmares being properly processed, so the anxiety and low self-esteem they generate does not reduce over time. Treatment of PTSD results in proper processing of the memories so, over time, the flashbacks and nightmares can gradually disappear. Clearly, how memory is categorized in your brain is complex and takes God to understand it.

How can you be permanently healed of those ugly memories? More than any psychological counseling, your heart and mind must be healed by

Jesus. Everyone has the same need for healing of some past woundedness. Counseling over years helps but there are limited results. The key is to fix the interpretation of bad memories. That is done through shedding light on them- God's light. Only God can bring light to our darkened minds. He does this through the words of the Bible, which He gave to us as a gift. Unless Jesus chooses to act and heal, likely no significant cure can occur. He reveals the truth. You must move aside and let the Holy Spirit expose your dark memories with light. Only He can set you free from lifelong fears, shame, false guilt, anxiety, depression, or PTSD.

God gave you a sophisticated brain with incredible abilities. He knew you would form memories, mostly good but some bad mixed in. He knew it would take a regular renewal of your mind to battle against memories of some of your wretched experiences in the past. He instructs us in four ways on how to *focus on him*. Meditate on these key points to help you have good memories:

1. Build up your memory bank with the attributes of God to know him better
Deuteronomy 8:2- *Remember* how the Lord your God led you all the way in the desert these forty years….
2. Renew your mind every day of your life. God will help you with this.
 Romans 12:2- Do not be conformed any longer to the pattern of this world but be transformed by the *renewing of your mind*.
3. Think about things that are excellent and praiseworthy.
Philippians 4:8 - Whatever is true, noble, right, pure, lovely, admirable, if anything is excellent or praiseworthy *think about such things*.
4. Establish your mind on the gifts of the Spirit- love, joy, peace, patience, kindness, goodness, faithfulness, gentleness, and self-control.
Colossians 3:2 *Set your minds* on things above, not on earthly things. For you died, and your life is now hidden with Christ in God. When Christ, who is your life, appears, then you also will appear with him in glory.

God does not want his people to forget him or what he has done for them. After He saved the first-born children during the first Passover (read **Exodus 11-13**), the Israelites were told to repeat the ceremony every year to reinforce the *memory* of God's grace. At the Lord's Supper, Jesus established a new ordinance: "Do this in *remembrance* of me" (read **Luke 22:19**). Every time we partake of communion at church, we *remember* his shed blood and the first observance in the upper room of Jesus and his disciples in Jerusalem. This God-ordained ceremony reinforces our *memory* of God's grace.

Of all your memories stored in your brain, God wants you to remember him preeminently and what He has accomplished for you through his Son, Jesus. Be unshackled from the prison chains of bad memories.

Key verses for your memory:

Psalm 22:27 All the ends of the earth will remember and turn to the Lord, and all the families of the nations will bow down before Him.
Psalm 145:7 They shall celebrate the memories of Your (God's) abundant goodness and joyfully sing of Your righteousness.

19 | Psalms for Wellness

(Learning to Go to God First)

WHEN YOU WANT TO REACH OUT TO GOD:

When you want to call out to God

5:1-2 Give ear to my words, O Lord, consider my sighing. Listen to my cry for help, my King and my God, for to You I pray.

6:6-7 I am worn out from groaning; all night long I flood my bed with weeping and drench my couch with tears. My eyes grow weak with sorrow; they fail because of all my foes.

31:16-17 Let Your face shine on your servant; save me in Your unfailing love. Let me not be put to shame, O Lord, for I have cried out to You.

66:16 Come and listen, all you who fear God; let me tell you what He has done for me. I cried out to Him with my mouth; His praise was on my tongue.

69:1-3 Save me, O God, for the waters have come up to my neck. I sink in the miry depths, where there is no foothold. I have come into the deep waters; the floods engulf me. I am worn out calling for help; my throat is parched. My eyes fail, looking for my God.

86:5 You are forgiving and good, O Lord, abounding in love to all who call to you.

88:1-2 O Lord, the God who saves me, day and night I cry out before You. May my prayer come before You; turn Your ear to my cry.

91:14-16 "Because he loves me", says the Lord, "I will rescue him; I will protect him, for he acknowledges my name. He will call upon me, and I will answer him; I will be with him in trouble, I will deliver him and honor him. With long life will I satisfy him and show him My salvation.

116:2 Because He turned His ear to me, I will call on Him as long as I live.

119:147 I rise before dawn and cry for help; I have put my hope in Your word.

142:5 I cry to you, O Lord; I say "You are my refuge, my portion in the land of the living."

143:1 O Lord, hear my prayer, listen to my cry for mercy; in Your faithfulness and righteousness come to my relief.

145:18 The Lord is near to all who call on Him, to all who call on Him in truth.

When you desire God

73:25 Who have I in heaven but you? And earth has nothing I desire besides You.

When you want to seek God

4:3b The Lord *will* hear when I call to Him.

14:2 The Lord looks down from heaven to see if there are any who seek God

16:6 I have set the Lord always before me. Because He is at my right hand, I will not be shaken.

17:1 Hear, O Lord, my righteous please; listen to my cry. Give ear to my prayer—

17:6 I call on You, O God, for You will answer me; give ear to me and hear my prayer.

18:3 I call to the Lord, who is worthy of praise, and I am saved from my enemies.

18:4-6 The cords of death entangled me; the torrents of destruction overwhelmed me. The cords of the grave coiled around me; the snares of death confronted me. In my distress I called to the Lord; I cried to my God for help. From His temple He heard my voice; my cry came before Him, into His ears.

27:7-9 Hear my voice when I call, O Lord; be merciful to me and answer me. My hear says of You, "Seek His face!" Your face, Lord, I will seek. Do not hide Your face from me, do not turn Your servant away in anger; You have been my helper. Do not reject me or forsake me, O God my Savior.

34:9 Fear the Lord, you His saints, for those who seek the Lord lack no good thing.

40:16 But may all who seek You rejoice and be glad in You; may those who love Your salvation always say, "The Lord be exalted!"

42:1-2 As the deer pants for streams of water, so my soul pants for You, O God. My soul thirsts for God, for the living God. When can I go and meet with God?

55:16-18 But I call to God, and the Lord saves me. Evening, morning, and noon I cry out in distress, and He hears my voice. He ransoms me unharmed from the battle wages against me, even though may oppose me.

55:22 Cast your cares on the Lord and He will sustain you; He will never let the righteous fall.

60:11-12 Give us aid against the enemy, for the help of man is worthless. With God we will gain the victory, and He will trample down our enemies.

63:1 O God, You are my God, earnestly I seek You; my soul thirsts for You, my body longs for You, in a dry and weary land where there is no water.

69:1-3 Save me, O God, for the waters have come up to my neck. I sink in the miry depths, where there is no foothold. I have come into the deep waters; the floods engulf me. I am worn out calling for help; my throat is parched. My eyes fail, looking for my God.

91:14-16 "Because he loves me", says the Lord, "I will rescue him; I will protect him, for he acknowledges My name. He will call upon me, and I will answer him; I will be with him in trouble, I will deliver him and honor him. With long life will I satisfy him and show him My salvation.

105:4 Look to the Lord and His strength; seek His face always.

When you want to confess to God

32:5 I acknowledged my sin to You and did not cover up my iniquity. I said, "I will confess my transgressions to the Lord"- and You forgave the guilt of my sin.

When you want to listen to God

81:8-10a Hear, O my people, and I will warn you- if you would but listen to Me (God). You shall have no foreign god among you; you shall not bow down to an alien god; I am the Lord your God.
85:8 I will listen to what God the Lord will say; He promises peace to His people

When you want to pray to God

4:1 Answer me when I call to You, O my righteous God, give me relief from my distress; be merciful to me and hear my prayer.
54:1-2 Save me, O God, by Your name; vindicate me by Your might. Hear my prayer, O God; listen to the words of my mouth.
61:1 Hear my cry, O God; listen to my prayer.
66:18-19 If I had cherished sin in my heart, the Lord would not have listened; but God has surely listened and heard my voice in prayer.
66:20 Praise be to God, who has not rejected my prayer or withheld His love from me!
67:5-7 May the peoples praise You, O God; may all the peoples praise You. Then the land will yield its harvest, and God, our God, will bless us. God will bless us, and all the ends of the earth will fear Him.
69:13 But I pray to you, O Lord, in the time of Your favor; in your great love, O God, answer me with Your sure salvation.
84:8 Hear my prayer, O Lord God Almighty; listen to me, O God of Jacob.
88:1-2 O Lord, the God who saves me, day and night I cry out before You. May my prayer come before You; turn Your ear to my cry.
88:13 But I cry to You for help, O Lord; in the morning my prayer comes before You.

When you want to trust in God

13:5 But I trust in Your unfailing love; my heart rejoices in Your salvation.
20:7 Some trust in chariots and some in horses, but we trust in the name of the Lord our God.
22:6, 8 But I am a worm and not a man, scorned by men and despised by the people. He trusts in the Lord; let the Lord rescue him. Let Him deliver him, since he delights in Him.
25:1 To you, O Lord, I lift up my soul; in You I trust, O my God.
28:7 The Lord is my strength and my shield; my heart trusts in Him, and I am helped. My heart leaps for joy and I will give thanks to Him in song.
31:14 But I trust in You, Lord; I say, "You are my God."
37:2 Trust in the Lord and do good; dwell in the land and enjoy safe pasture.

40:3b-4a Many will see and fear and put their trust in the Lord. Blessed is the person who makes the Lord his trust

52:8 But I am like an olive tree flourishing in the house of God; I trust in God's unfailing love for ever and ever.

56:3-4 When I am afraid, I will trust in You. In God, whose word I praise, in God I trust; I will not be afraid. What can mortal man do to me?

62:8 Trust in God at all times, O people; pour out your hearts to Him, for God is our refuge.

84:12 O Lord Almighty, blessed is the person who trusts in You.

86:2 Guard my life, for I am devoted to You. You are my God; save Your servant who trusts in You.

91:2 I will say of the Lord, "He is my refuge and my fortress, my God, in whom I trust."

143:8 Let the morning bring me word of Your unfailing love, for I have put my trust in You. Show me the way I should go, for to You I lift up my soul.

When you want hope in God

65:5 You answer us with awesome deeds of righteousness, O God our Savior, the hope of all the ends of the earth and of the farthest seas.

71:5 For You have been my hope, O Sovereign Lord, my confidence since my youth.

119:49 Remember Your word to Your servant, for You have given me hope.

119:147 I rise before dawn and cry for help; I have put my hope in Your word.

146:5-6 Blessed is the person whose help is God and whose hope is in the Lord their God, the Maker of heaven and earth, the sea, and everything in them—The Lord, who remains faithful forever.

147:11 The Lord delights in those who fear Him, who put their hope in His unfailing love.

When you are lonely

25:16 Turn to me and be gracious to me, for I am lonely and afflicted.

139:7-11 Where can I go from Your Spirit? Where can I flee from Your presence? If I go up to the heavens, You are there; if I make my bed in the depths, You are there. If I rise on the wings of the dawn, if I settle on the far side of the sea, even there Your hand will guide me, Your right hand will hold me fast. If I say, "Surely the darkness will hide me and the light become night around me," even the darkness will not be dark to You; the night will shine like the day, for darkness is as light to You.

WHEN YOU ARE STRUGGLING:

When you are afflicted

10:12, 17-18 Arise, Lord! Lift Your hand, O God. Do not forget the helpless. You hear, O Lord, the desire of the afflicted; You encourage them, and You listen to their cry, defending the fatherless and the oppressed, in order that man, who is of the earth, may terrify no more.
25:16-18 Turn to me and be gracious to me, for I am lonely and afflicted. The troubles of my heart have multiplied; free me from my anguish. Look upon my affliction and my distress and take away all my sins.
40:17 Yet I am poor and needy; may the Lord think of me. You are my help and my deliverer; O my God, do not delay.
72:4 God will defend the afflicted among the people and save the children of the needy; He will crush the oppressor.
119:71 It was good for me to be afflicted so that I might learn Your decrees.
119:92 If Your law had not been my delight, I would have perished in my affliction.

When you are in agony

6:2 Be merciful to me, Lord, for I am faint; O Lord, heal me, for my bones are in agony. My soul is in anguish. How long, O Lord, how long?
57:1 Have mercy on me, O God, have mercy on me, for in you my soul takes refuge. I will take refuge in the shadow of Your wings until the disaster has passed.

When you are struggling with anger

4:4 In your anger do not sin; when you are on your beds, search your hearts and be silent.
37:8 Refrain from anger and turn from wrath; do not fret –it leads only to evil.

When you are thinking about death

55:4-8 My heart is in anguish within me; the terrors of death assail me. Fear and trembling have beset me; horror has overwhelmed me. I said, "Oh, that I had the wings of a dove! I would fly far away and stay in the desert; I would hurry to my place of shelter, far from the tempest and storm."
56:13 For You have delivered me from death and my feet from stumbling, that I may walk before God in the light of life.
86:13 For great is Your love toward me; You have delivered me from the depths of the grave.
88:3 For my soul is full of trouble and my life draws near the grave. I am counted among those who go down to the pit; I am like a person without strength.
94:17 Unless the Lord had given me help, I would soon have dwelt in the silence of death.

116:3-4 The cords of death entangled me, the anguish of the grave came upon me; I was overcome by trouble and sorrow. Then I called on the name of the Lord; "O Lord, save me!"

When you are depressed

6:2 Be merciful to me, Lord, for I am faint; O Lord, heal me, for my bones are in agony. My soul is in anguish. How long, O Lord, how long?
6:6-7 I am worn out from groaning; all night long I flood my bed with weeping and drench my couch with tears. My eyes grow weak with sorrow; they fail because of all my foes.
13:2 How long must I wrestle with my thoughts and every day have sorrow in my heart? How long will my enemy triumph over me?
69:1-3 Save me, O God, for the waters have come up to my neck. I sink in the miry depths, where there is no foothold. I have come into the deep waters; the floods engulf me. I am worn out calling for help; my throat is parched. My eyes fail, looking for my God.

When you are in distress

4:1 Answer me when I call to you, O my righteous God, give me relief from my distress; be merciful to me and hear my prayer.
20:1 May the Lord answer you when you are in distress; may the name of the God of Jacob protect you.
31:9-10 Be merciful to me, O Lord, for I am in distress; my eyes grow weak with sorrow, my soul and my body with grief. My life is consumed by anguish and my years by groaning; my strength fails because of my affliction, and my bones grow weak.
39:12 "Hear my prayer, O Lord, listen to my cry for help; be not deaf to my weeping."
42:5 Why are you downcast, O my soul? Why so disturbed within me? Put your hope in God, for I will yet praise Him, my Savior and my God.
55:1-2 Listen to my prayer, O God, do not ignore my plea; hear me and answer me. My thoughts trouble me and I am distraught.
56:8 Record my lament; list my tears on your scroll- are they not in your record?
59:16-17 I will sing of Your strength, in the morning I will sing of Your love; for You are my fortress, my refuge in times of trouble. O my Strength, I sing praise to You; You, O God, are my fortress, my loving God.
69:29 I am in pain and distress; may Your salvation, O God, protect me.
77:2 When I was in distress, I sought the Lord; at night I stretched out untiring hands and my soul refused to be comforted.
107:5-6 They were hungry and thirsty, and their lives ebbed away. Then they cried out to the Lord in their trouble, and He delivered them from their distress.
119:143 Trouble and distress have come upon me, but Your commands are my delight.
120:1 I call on the Lord in my distress, and He answers me.

When you are afraid

3:6 I will not fear that tens of thousands drawn up against me on every side.
7:1 O Lord God, I take refuge in You; save and deliver me from all who pursue me, or they will tear me like a lion.
10:12, 17-18 Arise, Lord! Lift Your hand, O God. Do not forget the helpless. You hear, O Lord, the desire of the afflicted; You encourage them, and You listen to their cry, defending the fatherless and the oppressed, in order that man, who is of the earth, may terrify no more.
16:9-10 Therefore my heart is glad (because I have set the Lord always before me and therefore I am not shaken) and my tongue rejoices; my body also will rest secure, because You will not abandon me to the grave, nor will You let your Holy One see decay.
23:4 Even though I walk through the valley of the shadow of death, I will fear no evil, for You are with me; Your rod and Your staff, they comfort me.
27:1 The Lord is my light and my salvation—who should I fear? The Lord is the stronghold of my life—of whom shall I be afraid?
27:13-14 I am still confident of this; I will see the goodness of the Lord in the land of the living.
34:4 I sought the Lord, and He answered me; He delivered me from all my fears. The angel of the Lord encamps around those who fear Him, and He delivers them.
41:12 In my integrity You uphold me and set me in your presence forever.
46:2 Therefore we will not fear, though the earth gives way and the mountains fall into the heart of the seas, though its waters roar and foam and the mountains quake with their surging.
56:3-4 When I am afraid, I will trust in You. In God, whose word I praise, in God I trust; I will not be afraid. What can mortal man do to me?
91:5-7 You will not fear the terror of night, nor the arrow that flies by day, nor the pestilence that stalks in the darkness, nor the plague that destroys at midday. A thousand may fall at your side, ten thousand at your right and, but it will not come near you.
112:7 He will have no fear of bad news; his heart is steadfast, trusting in the Lord.

When you are dealing with guilt

25:6-7 Remember, O Lord, your great mercy and love, for they are from of old. Remember not the sins of my youth and my rebellious ways; according to Your love remember me, for You are good, O Lord.
32:5 I acknowledged my sin to You and did not cover up my iniquity. I said, "I will confess my transgressions to the Lord"- and You forgave the guilt of my sin.

When you are sick

6:2 Be merciful to me, Lord, for I am faint; O Lord, heal me, for my bones are in agony. My soul is in anguish. How long, O Lord, how long?

41:4 I said, "O Lord, have mercy on me; heal me, for I have sinned against You."
102:3-6 For my days vanish like smoke; my bones burn like glowing embers. My heart is blighted and withered like grass; I forget to eat my food. Because of my loud groaning I am reduced to skin and bones. I am like a desert owl, like an owl among the ruins.
103:3-4 God forgives all your sins and heals all your disease, who redeems your life from the pit and crowns you with love and compassion.
107:20 He sent forth His word and healed them; He rescued them from the grave.
119:82 My eyes fail, looking for Your promise; I say, "When will you comfort me?"
119:123 My eyes fail, looking for Your salvation, looking for Your righteous promise.
147:3 God heals the brokenhearted and binds up their wounds.

When you are dealing with sin

40:12 For troubles without number surround me; my sins have overtaken me, and I cannot see. They are more than the hairs of my head, and my heart fails within me.
51:1-2 Have mercy on me, O God, according to Your unfailing love; according to Your great compassion blot out my transgressions. Wash away all my iniquity and cleanse me from my sin.
85:2 You (God) forgave the iniquity of Your people and covered all their sins.
103:12 As far as the east is from the west, so far has He removed our transgressions from us.
106:6, 8 We have sinned, even as our fathers did; we have done wrong and acted wickedly. Yet God saves us for His names' sake, to make His mighty power known.
130:3-4 If you, O Lord, kept a record of sins, O Lord, who could stand? But with You there is forgiveness

When you are in trouble

40:12 For troubles without number surround me; my sins have overtaken me, and I cannot see. They are more than the hairs of my head, and my heart fails within me.
46:1 God is our refuge and strength, an ever-present help in trouble.
50:15 God says, "Call upon me in the day of trouble; I will deliver you, and you will honor Me."
55:1-2 Listen to my prayer, O God, do not ignore my plea; hear me and answer me. My thoughts trouble me and I am distraught.
69:16-17 Answer me, O Lord, out of the goodness of Your love; in Your great mercy turn to me. Do not hide Your face from Your servant; answer me quickly, for I am in trouble.
86:6-7 Hear my prayer, O Lord; listen to my cry for mercy, in the day of my trouble I will call to You, for You will answer me.

88:3 For my soul is full of trouble and my life draws near the grave. I am counted among those who go down to the pit; I am like a person without strength.
119:50 My comfort in my suffering is this; Your promise preserves my life.
119:153 Look upon my suffering and deliver me, for I have not forgotten Your law.
138:7 Though I walk in the middle of trouble, You preserve my life
142:3 When my spirit grows faint within me, it is You who know my way.
143:4 So my spirits grows faint within me; my heart within me is dismayed.
143:11 For Your name's sake, O Lord, preserve my life; in Your righteousness, bring me out of trouble.

When you are weary

119:28 My soul is weary with sorrow; strengthen me according to Your word.
143:4 So my spirits grow faint within me; my heart within me is dismayed.

When you are worried

37:7 Be still before the Lord and wait patiently for Him; do not fret when mend succeed in their ways, when they carry out their wicked schemes.
94:19 When anxiety was great within me, Your consolation brings joy to my soul.

When you are straying

119:176 I have strayed like a lost sheep. Seek Your servant, for I have not forgotten Your commands.

WHEN THINGS ARE GOING WELL (don't forget about God):

When you are feeling blessed

1:1 Blessed is the person who does not walk in the counsel of the wicked or stand in the way of sinners or sit in the seat of mockers.
2:12b Blessed are all who take refuge in the Lord.
5:11 But let all who take refuge in You be glad; let them every sing for joy. Spread Your protection over them, that those who love Your name may rejoice in You. For surely, O Lord, You bless the righteous; You surround them with Your favor as with a shield.
28:8-9 The Lord is the strength of His people, a fortress of salvation for His anointed one. Save Your people and bless Your inheritance; be their shepherd and carry them forever.

32: 1-2 Blessed is the person whose transgressions are forgiven, whose sins are covered, and whose sin the Lord does not count against Him and in whose spirit is no deceit.
34:8 Taste and see that the Lord is good; blessed is the man who takes refuge in Him.
67:1 May God be gracious to us and bless us and make His face shine upon us.
84:5 Blessed are those whose strength is in You.
84:12 O Lord Almighty, blessed is the person who trusts in You.
146:5-6 Blessed is the person whose help is God and whose hope is in the Lord their God, the Maker of heaven and earth, the sea, and everything in them — The Lord, who remains faithful forever.

When you are feeling content

16:5a Lord, You have assigned me my portion and my cup You have made my lot secure.
23:1 The Lord is my Shepherd, I shall not be in want.

When you are full of delight

1:2-3 Your delight is in the law of the Lord, and on the Scripture he meditates day and night. He is like a tree planted by streams of water, which yields its fruit in season and whose leaf does not wither. Whatever he does prospers.
37:4 Delight yourself in the Lord and He will give you the desires of your heart.

When you want to show devotion to God

86:2 Guard my life, for I am devoted to You. You are my God; save Your servant who trusts in You.

When you are thinking about eternity

52:8 But I am like an olive tree flourishing in the house of God; I trust in God's unfailing love for ever and ever.
73:24 You guide me with Your counsel, and afterward You will take me into glory.
73:26 My flesh and my heart may fail, but God is the strength of my heart and my portion forever.

When you are feeling glad to know God

5:11-12 But let all who take refuge in You be glad; let them ever sing for joy. Spread Your protection over them, that those who love Your name may rejoice in You.
9:1-2 I will praise You, O Lord, with all my heart; I will tell of all Your wonders. I will be glad and rejoice in You; I will sing praise to Your name, O Most High.
16:9 Therefore my heart is glad (because I have set the Lord always before me and therefore I am not shaken) and my tongue rejoices; my body also will rest

secure, because You will not abandon me to the grave, nor will you let Your Holy One see decay.

31:7 I will be glad and rejoice in Your love, for You saw my affliction and knew the anguish of my soul.

40:16 But may all who seek You rejoice and be glad in You; may those who love Your salvation always say, "The Lord be exalted!"

When you have joy

4:7 You (the Lord) have filled my heart with greater joy than when their grain and new wine abound.

5:11 But let all who take refuge in You be glad; let them every sing for joy. Spread Your protection over them, that those who love Your name may rejoice in You. For surely, O Lord, You bless the righteous; You surround them with Your favor as with a shield.

16:11 You God have made known to me the path of life; You will fill me with joy in Your presence, with eternal pleasures at Your right hand.

19:8 The precepts of the Lord are right, giving joy to the heart. The commands of the Lord are radiant, giving light to the eyes.

21:6 Surely you have granted Him eternal blessings and made him glad with joy of Your presence.

28:7 The Lord is my strength and my shield; my heart trusts in Him, and I am helped. My heart leaps for joy and I will give thanks to Him in song.

30:11-12 You turned my wailing into dancing; You removed my sackcloth and clothed me with joy, that my heart may sing to You and not be silent. Lord my God, I will give You thanks forever.

31:7 I will be glad and rejoice in Your love, for You saw my affliction and knew the anguish of my soul.

33:1-3 Sing joyfully to the Lord, you righteous; it is fitting for the upright to praise Him. Praise the Lord with the harp; make music to Him on the ten-stringed lyre. Sing to Him a new song; play skillfully, and shout for joy.

51:10-12 Create in me a pure heart, O God, and renew a steadfast spirit within me. Do not cast me from Your presence or take Your Holy Spirit from me. Restore to me the joy of Your salvation and grant me a willing spirit, to sustain me.

90:14 Satisfy us in the morning with Your unfailing love, that we may sing for joy and be glad all our days.

94:19 When anxiety was great within me, Your consolation brought joy to my soul.

95:1-2 Come, let us sing for joy to the Lord; let us shout aloud to the Rock of our salvation. Let us come before Him with thanksgiving and extol Him with music and song.

WHEN YOU WANT TO PRAISE GOD:

When you have awe for God

25:12-14 Who, then, is the man that fears the Lord? He will instruct Him in the way chosen for Him. He will spend his days in prosperity, and his descendants will inherit the land. The Lord confides in those who fear Him; He makes His covenant known to them.

31:19 How great is Your goodness, which you have stored up for those who fear You, which You bestow in the sight of men on those who take refuge in You.

33:8 Let all the earth fear the Lord; let all the people of the world revere Him.

33:18-19 But the eyes of the Lord are on those who fear Him, on those whose hope is in His unfailing love, to deliver them from death and keep them alive in famine.

34:4 I sought the Lord, and He answered me; He delivered me from all my fears. The angel of the Lord encamps around those who fear Him, and He delivers them.

34:9 Fear the Lord, you his saints, for those who seek the Lord lack no good thing.

66:16 Come and listen, all you who fear God; let me tell you what He has done for me. I cried out to Him with my mouth; His praise was on my tongue.

67:5-7 May the peoples praise You, O God; may all the peoples praise You. Then the land will yield its harvest, and God, our God, will bless us. God will bless us, and all the ends of the earth will fear Him.

85:9 Surely His salvation is near those who fear Him, that His glory may dwell in our land.

96:4 For great is the Lord and most worthy of praise; He is to be feared above all gods.

103:11 For as high as the heavens are above the earth, so great is His love for those who fear (have awe for) Him

103:13-14 As a father has compassion on his children, so the Lord has compassion on those who fear Him; for He knows how we were formed, He remembers that we are dust.

103:17 But from everlasting to everlasting the Lord's love is with those who fear Him, and His righteousness with their children's children- with those who keep His covenant and remember to obey His precepts.

111:10 The fear of the Lord is the beginning of wisdom; all who follow His precepts have good understanding. To Him belongs eternal praise.

112:1 Praise the Lord. Blessed is the person who fears the Lord, who finds great delight in His commands.

115:11 You who fear Him, trust in the Lord—He is their help and shield.

115:13 He will bless those who fear the Lord—small and great alike.

145:19 God fulfills the desires of those who fear Him; He hears their cry and saves them.

147:11 The Lord delights in those who fear Him, who put their hope in his unfailing love.

When you have hope in God

25:4-5 Show me Your ways, O Lord, teach me Your paths; guide me in Your truth and teach me, for You are God my Savior, and my hope is in You all day long.
25:21 May integrity and uprightness protect me, because my hope is in You.
31:24 Be strong and take heart, all you who hope in the Lord.
33:18-19 But the eyes of the Lord are on those who fear Him, on those whose hope is in His unfailing love, to deliver them from death and keep them alive in famine.
33:20 We wait in hope for the Lord; He is our help and our shield.
33:22 May your unfailing love rest upon us, O Lord, even as we put our hope in You.
39:7 "But now, Lord, what do I look for? My hope is in You."
42:5, 11, 43:5 Why are you downcast, O my soul? Why so disturbed within me? Put your hope in God, for I will yet praise Him, my Savior and my God.
62:5 Find rest, O my soul, in God alone; my hope come from Him.
71:14 But as for me, I will always have hope; I will praise You more and more.
119:114 You are my refuge and my shield; I have put my hope in Your word.
119:147 I rise before dawn and cry for help; I have put my hope in Your word.
130:5 I wait for the Lord, my soul waits, and in His word I put my hope.

When you want to love God

91:14-16 "Because he loves me", says the Lord, "I will rescue him; I will protect him, for he acknowledges My name. He will call upon me, and I will answer him; I will be with him in trouble, I will deliver him and honor him. With long life will I satisfy him and show him My salvation.
145:20 The Lord watches over all who love Him

When you want to praise God

8:1-2, 9 O Lord, our Lord, how majestic is Your name in all the earth! You have set Your glory above the heavens.
9:1-2 I will praise you, O Lord, with all my heart; I will tell of all Your wonders. I will be glad and rejoice in You; I will sing praise to Your name, O Most High.
16:7 I will praise the Lord, who counsels me; even at night my heart instructs me.
18:3 I call to the Lord, who is worthy of praise, and I am saved from my enemies.
18:46, 49 The Lord lives! Praise be to my Rock! Exalted be God my Savior! I will praise You among the nations, O Lord; I will sing praises to Your name.
21:13 Be exalted, O Lord, in Your strength; we will sing and praise Your might.
26:6b-7 I go about your altar, O Lord, proclaiming aloud Your praise and telling of all Your wonderful deeds.
28:6 Praise be to the Lord, for He has heard my cry for mercy.
29:1-2 Ascribe to the Lord glory and strength. Ascribe to the Lord the glory due His name; worship the Lord in the splendor of His holiness.

30:1-3 I will exalt you, O Lord, for You lifted me out of the depths and did not let my enemies gloat over me. O Lord my God, I called to You for help and You healed me. O Lord, You brought me up from the grave; You spared me from going down into the pit.

31:21 Praise be to the Lord, for He showed His wonderful love to me when I was in a besieged city.

33:1-3 Sing joyfully to the Lord, you righteous; it is fitting for the upright to praise Him. Praise the Lord with the harp; make music to Him on the ten-stringed lyre. Sing to Him a new song; play skillfully, and shout for joy.

35:27-28 May the Lord be exalted, who delights in the well-being of His servant. My tongue will speak of Your righteousness and of Your praises all day long.

40:3 God put a new song in my mouth, a hymn of praise to our God.

40:16 But may all who seek You rejoice and be glad in You; may those who love Your salvation always say, "The Lord be exalted!"

41:13 Praise be to the Lord, the God of Israel, from everlasting to everlasting.

42:5 Why are you downcast, O my soul? Why so disturbed within me? Put your hope in God, for I will yet praise Him, my Savior and my God.

46:10 Be still and know that I am God; I will be exalted among the nations, I will be exalted in the earth.

48:1 Great is the Lord, and most worth of praise, in the city of our God, His holy mountain.

56:3-4 When I am afraid, I will trust in You (God). In God, whose word I praise, in God I trust; I will not be afraid. What can mortal man do to me?

56:10-11 In God, whose word I praise, in the Lord, whose word I praise—in God I trust; I will not be afraid. What can man do to me?

57:5,11 Be exalted, O God, above the heavens; let Your glory be over all the earth (despite hardships).

59:16-17 I will sing of Your (God's) strength, in the morning I will sing of Your love; for You are my fortress, my refuge in times of trouble. O my Strength, I sing praise to You; You, O God, are my fortress, my loving God.

63:4 I will praise You (God) as long as I live, and in Your name I will lift up my hands.

63:5 My soul will be satisfied as with the richest of foods; with singing lips my mouth will praise You.

64:10 Let the righteous rejoice in the Lord and take refuge in Him; let all the upright in heart praise Him.

66:8-9 Praise our God, O people, let the sound of His praise be heard; He has preserved our lives and kept our feet from slipping.

66:16 Come and listen, all you who fear God; let me tell you what He has done for me. I cried out to Him with my mouth; His praise was on my tongue.

66:20 Praise be to God, who has not rejected my prayer or withheld His love from me!

68:19 Praise be to the Lord, to God our Savior, who daily bears our burdens.

69:30 I will praise God's name in song and glorify Him with thanksgiving.

71:14 But as for me, I will always have hope; I will praise You more and more.

71:16 I will proclaim Your mighty acts, O Sovereign Lord; I will proclaim Your righteousness, Yours alone.

71:17 Since my youth, O God, You have taught me, and to this day I declare Your marvelous deeds.

71:18 Even when I am old and gray, do not forsake me, O God, till I declare Your power to the next generation, Your might to all who are to come.

71:22 I will praise You with the harp for Your faithfulness, O my God; I will sing praise to You with the lyre

71:23-24 My lips will shout for joy when I sing praise to You-I, whom You have redeemed. My tongue will tell of Your righteous acts all day long

89:5 The heavens praise Your wonders, O Lord, Your faithfulness too, in the assembly of the holy ones.

92:1-3 It is good to praise the Lord and make music to Your name, O Most High, to proclaim Your love in the morning and Your faithfulness at night, to the music of the ten-stringed lyre and the melody of the harp.

95:1-2 Come, let us sing for joy to the Lord; let us shout aloud to the Rock of our salvation. Let us come before Him with thanksgiving and extol Him with music and song.

96:1-2 Sing to the Lord a new song; sing to the Lord, all the earth. Sing to the Lord, praise His name; proclaim His salvation day after day.

96:3 Declare His glory among the nations, His marvelous deeds among all peoples.

96:4 For great is the Lord and most worthy of praise; He is to be feared above all gods.

97:9 For you, O Lord, are the most High over all the earth; You are exalted far above all gods.

101:1 I will sing of Your love and justice; to You, O Lord, I will sing praise.

142:7 Set me free from my prison, that I may praise Your name.

When you want to rejoice in God

9:1-2 I will praise you, O Lord, with all my heart; I will tell of all Your wonders. I will be glad and rejoice in You; I will sing praise to Your name, O Most High.

13:5 But I trust in Your unfailing love; my heart rejoices in Your salvation.

16:9-10 Therefore my heart is glad (because I have set the Lord always before me and therefore I am not shaken) and my tongue rejoices; my body also will rest secure, because You will not abandon me to the grave, nor will You let Your Holy One see decay.

31:7 I will be glad and rejoice in Your love, for You saw my affliction and knew the anguish of my soul.

32:11 Rejoice in the Lord and be glad, you righteous; sing, all you who are upright in heart!

89:15-16 Blessed are those who have learned to acclaim You, who walk in the light of Your presence, O Lord. They rejoice in Your name all day long; they exalt in Your righteousness.

118:24 This is the day that the Lord has made; let us rejoice and be glad in it.

When you want to sing to God

7:17 I will give thanks to the Lord because of His righteousness and will sing praise to the name of the Lord Most High.

9:1-2 I will praise you, O Lord, with all my heart; I will tell of all Your wonders. I will be glad and rejoice in You; I will sing praise to Your name, O Most High.

13:6 I will sing to the Lord, for He has been good to me.

18:46, 49 The Lord lives! Praise be to my Rock! Exalted be God my Savior! I will praise You among the nations, O Lord; I will sing praises to Your name.

21:13 Be exalted, O Lord, in Your strength; we will sing and praise Your might.

28:7 The Lord is my strength and my shield; my heart trusts in Him, and I am helped. My heart leaps for joy and I will give thanks to Him in song.

30:4 Sing to the Lord, you saints of His; praise His holy name.

30:11-12 You turned my wailing into dancing; You removed my sackcloth and clothed me with joy, that my heart may sing to You and not be silent. Lord my God, I will give You thanks forever.

32:11 Rejoice in the Lord and be glad, You righteous; sing, all you who are upright in heart!

33:1-3 Sing joyfully to the Lord, you righteous; it is fitting for the upright to praise Him. Praise the Lord with the harp; make music to Him on the ten-stringed lyre. Sing to Him a new song; play skillfully, and shout for joy.

40:3 God put a new song in my mouth, a hymn of praise to our God.

57:7 My heart is steadfast, O God, my heart is steadfast; I will sing and make music, Awake, my soul!

59:16-17 I will sing of Your (God's) strength, in the morning I will sing of Your love; for You are my fortress, my refuge in times of trouble. O my Strength, I sing praise to You; You, O God, are my fortress, my loving God.

63:7 Because You are my help, I sing in the shadow of Your wings.

69:30 I will praise God's name in song and glorify Him with thanksgiving.

71:22 I will praise You with the harp for Your faithfulness, O my God; I will sing praise to You with the lyre

71:23-24 My lips will shout for joy when I sing praise to You-I, whom You have redeemed. My tongue will tell of Your righteous acts all day long

89:1 I will sing of the Lord's great love forever; with my mouth I will make Your faithfulness known through all generations. I will declare that Your love stands firm forever, that You established Your faithfulness in heaven itself.

90:14 Satisfy us in the morning with Your unfailing love, that we may sing for joy and be glad all our days.

95:1-2 Come, let us sing for joy to the Lord; let us shout aloud to the Rock of our salvation. Let us come before Him with thanksgiving and extol Him with music and song.

96:1-2 Sing to the Lord a new song; sing to the Lord, all the earth. Sing to the Lord, praise His name; proclaim His salvation day after day.

101:1 I will sing of Your love and justice; to You, O Lord, I will sing praise.

108:1 My heart is steadfast, O God; I will sing and make music with all my soul.

When you want to thank God

28:7 The Lord is my strength and my shield; my heart trusts in Him, and I am helped. My heart leaps for joy and I will give thanks to Him in song.

30:11-12 You turned my wailing into dancing; You removed my sackcloth and clothed me with joy, that my heart may sing to You and not be silent. Lord my God, I will give You thanks forever.

95:1-2 Come, let us sing for joy to the Lord; let us shout aloud to the Rock of our salvation. Let us come before Him with thanksgiving and extol Him with music and song.

WHEN YOU WANT TO EXAMINE YOURSELF:

When you want to examine your heart

9:1-2 I will praise you, O Lord, with all my heart; I will tell of all Your wonders. I will be glad and rejoice in You; I will sing praise to Your name, O Most High.
16:9 Therefore my heart is glad (because I have set the Lord always before me and therefore I am not shaken) and my tongue rejoices; my body also will rest secure, because You will not abandon me to the grave, nor will you let your Holy One see decay.
28:7 The Lord is my strength and my shield; my heart trusts in Him, and I am helped. My heart leaps for joy and I will give thanks to Him in song.
30:11-12 You turned my wailing into dancing; You removed my sackcloth and clothed me with joy, that my heart may sing to You and not be silent. Lord my God, I will give You thanks forever.
40:12 For troubles without number surround me; my sins have overtaken me, and I cannot see. They are more than the hairs of my head, and my heart fails within me.
51:10-12 Create in me a pure heart, O God, and renew a steadfast spirit within me. Do not cast me from Your presence or take Your Holy Spirit from me. Restore to me the joy of Your salvation and grant me a willing spirit, to sustain me.
57:7 My heart is steadfast, O God, my heart is steadfast; I will sing and make music, Awake, my soul!
61:2-3 For the ends of the earth I call to You, I call as my heart grows faint; lead me to the rock that is higher than I. For You have been my refuge, as strong tower against the foe.
66:18-19 If I had cherished sin in my heart, the Lord would not have listened; but God has surely listened and heard my voice in prayer.
73:26 My flesh and my heart may fail, but God is the strength of my heart and my portion forever.
84:2 My soul yearns, even faints, for the courts of the Lord; my heart and my flesh cry out for the living God.
108:1 My heart is steadfast, O God; I will sing and make music with all my soul.
109:21-22 But You, O Sovereign Lord, deal well with me for Your name's sake; out of the goodness of Your love, deliver me. For I am poor and needy, and my heart is wounded within me.
112:8 His heart is secure, he will have no fear; in the end he will look in triumph on his foes.
143:4 So my spirits grow faint within me; my heart within me is dismayed.

When you want to be humble before God

25:8-9 Good and upright is the Lord; therefor He instructs sinners in His ways. He guides the humble in what is right and teaches them His way.
119:25 I am laid low in the dust; preserve my life according to Your word.

When you want to enrich your soul

6:2 Be merciful to me, Lord, for I am faint; O Lord, heal me, for my bones are in agony. My soul is in anguish. How long, O Lord, how long?
19:7a The law of the Lord is perfect, reviving the soul.
23:2 He makes me lie down in green pastures, He leads me beside quiet waters, He restores my soul.
25:1 To you, O Lord, I lift up my soul; in You I trust, O my God.
31:7 I will be glad and rejoice in Your love, for You saw my affliction and knew the anguish of my soul.
31:9-10 Be merciful to me, O Lord, for I am in distress; my eyes grow weak with sorrow, my soul and my body with grief. My life is consumed by anguish and my years by groaning; my strength fails because of my affliction, and my bones grow weak.
34:1-3 I will extol the Lord at all times; His praise will always be on my lips. My soul will boast in the Lord; let the afflicted hear and rejoice. Glorify the Lord with me; let us exalt His name together.
42:1 As the deer pants for streams of water, so my soul pants for you, O God.
42:5, 11, 43:5 Why are you downcast, O my soul? Why so disturbed within me? Put your hope in God, for I will yet praise Him, my Savior and my God.
57:7 My heart is steadfast, O God, my heart is steadfast; I will sing and make music, Awake, my soul!
62:1 My soul finds rest in God alone; my salvation come from Him.
62:5 Find rest, O my soul, in God alone; my hope come from Him.
63:1 O God, You are my God, earnestly I seek You; my soul thirsts for You, my body longs for You, in a dry and weary land where there is no water.
63:5 My soul will be satisfied as with the richest of foods; with singing lips my mouth will praise You.
63:8 My soul clings to You; Your right hand upholds me.
77:2 When I was in distress, I sought the Lord; at night I stretched out untiring hands and my soul refused to be comforted.
84:2 My soul yearns, even faints, for the courts of the Lord; my heart and my flesh cry out for the living God.
86:4 Bring joy to Your servant, for to You, O Lord, I lift up my soul.
88:3 For my soul is full of trouble and my life draws near the grave. I am counted among those who go down to the pit; I am like a person without strength.
94:19 When anxiety was great within me, Your consolation brought joy to my soul.
108:1 My heart is steadfast, O God; I will sing and make music with all my soul.
116:7 Be at rest once more, O my soul, for the Lord has been good to you.
116:8 For you, O Lord, have delivered my soul from death, my eyes from tears, my feet from stumbling, that I may walk before the Lord

119:28 My soul is weary with sorrow; strengthen me according to Your word.
130:5 I wait for the Lord, my soul waits, and in His Word I put my hope.
143:6 I spread out my hands to You; my soul thirsts for You like a parched land.
143:8 Let the morning bring me word of Your unfailing love, for I have put my trust in You. Show me the way I should go, for to You I lift up my soul.

When you want to be still

16:9 Therefore my heart is glad (because I have set the Lord always before me and therefore I am not shaken) and my tongue rejoices; my body also will rest secure, because You will not abandon me to the grave, nor will You let your Holy One see decay.
33:22 May Your unfailing love rest upon us, O Lord, even as we put our hope in You.
37:7 Be still before the Lord and wait patiently for Him; do not fret when men succeed in their ways, when they carry out their wicked schemes.
46:10 Be still and know that I am God
91:1 He who dwells in the shelter of the Most High will rest in the shadow of the Almighty.

When you desire God's guidance

31:2-3 Turn Your ear to me, come quickly to my rescue; by my rock of refuge, a strong fortress to save me. Since You are my Rock and my fortress, for the sake of Your name lead and guide me.
48:14 For this God is our God for ever and ever; He will be our guide even to the end.
67:4 May the nations be glad and sing for joy, for You (God) rule the peoples justly and guide the nations of the earth.
73:24 You guide me with Your counsel, and afterward You will take me into glory.

When you are seeking God's will

143:10 Teach me to do Your will, for You are my God; may Your good Spirit lead me on level ground.

Knowing God Better Through the Psalms

GOD IS YOUR COMFORTER:

God cares for you

138:6 Though the Lord is on high, He looks upon the lowly, but the proud He knows from afar.
144:3 O Lord, what is man that You care for him, the son of man that You think of him? Man is like a breath; his days are like a fleeting shadow.

God is your comforter

23:4 Even though I walk through the valley of the shadow of death, I will fear no evil, for You are with me; Your rod and Your staff, they comfort me.
71:20-21 Though You have made me see troubles, many and bitter, You will restore my life again; from the depths of the earth You will again bring me up. You will increase my honor and comfort me once again.
86:17 Give me a sign of Your goodness, that my enemies may see it and be put to shame, for You, O Lord, have helped me and comforted me.
119:76 May Your unfailing love be my comfort, according to Your promise to Your servant.
119:82 My eyes fail, looking for Your promise; I say, "When will You comfort me?"

God has compassion for you

51:1-2 Have mercy on me, O God, according to Your unfailing love; according to Your great compassion blot out my transgressions. Wash away all my iniquity and cleanse me from my sin.
68:5-6 God, the father to the fatherless, a defender of widows, is God in His holy dwelling. God sets the lonely in families, He leads forth the prisoners with singing
86:15 But you, O Lord, are a compassionate and gracious God, slow to anger, abounding in love and faithfulness.
103:3-4 God forgives all your sins and heals all your disease, who redeems your life from the pit and crowns you with love and compassion.
103:8 the Lord is compassionate and gracious, slow to anger, abounding in love.
103:13-14 As a father has compassion on his children, so the Lord has compassion on those who fear Him; for He knows how we were formed, He remembers that we are dust.
111:4 He has caused his wonders to be remembered; the Lord is gracious and compassionate.
116:5 The Lord is gracious and righteous; our God is full of compassion.
119:77 Let your compassion come to me that I may live, for Your law is my delight.

119:156 Your compassion is great, O Lord; preserve my life according to Your laws.
145:8 The Lord is gracious and compassionate, slow to anger and rich in love.
145:9 The Lord is good to all; He has compassion on all He has made.

God counsels you

1:2-3 Your delight is in the law of the Lord, and on the Bible he meditates day and night. He is like a tree planted by streams of water, which yields its fruit in season and whose leaf does not wither. Whatever he does prospers.
16:7 I will praise the Lord, who counsels me; even at night my heart instructs me.
16:11 You God, have made known to me the path of life; You will fill me with joy in Your presence, with eternal pleasures at Your right hand.
25:4-5 Show me Your ways, O Lord, teach me Your paths; guide me in Your truth and teach me, for You are God my Savior, and my hope is in You all day long.
25:8-9 Good and upright is the Lord; therefor He instructs sinners in His ways. He guides the humble in what is right and teaches them His way.
25:12-13 Who, then, is the man that fears the Lord? He will instruct him in the way chosen for him. He will spend his days in prosperity, and his descendants will inherit the land.
32:8 I will instruct you and teach you in the way you should go; I will counsel you and watch over you.
71:17 Since my youth, O God, You have taught me, and to this day I declare Your marvelous deeds.
73:24 You guide me with Your counsel, and afterward You will take me into glory.
86:11 Teach me Your way, O Lord; and I will walk in Your truth.
94:12-13a Blessed is the man You discipline, O Lord, the man You teach from Your law; You grant him relief from days of trouble

106:13-15 But people soon forgot what God had done and did not wait for His counsel. In the desert, the Israelites gave in to their craving; in the wasteland they put God to the test. So he gave them what they asked for, but sent a wasting disease upon them.
143:10 Teach me to do Your will, for you are my God; may Your good Spirit lead me on level ground.

God's shows you mercy

4:1 Answer me when I call to you, O my righteous God, give me relief from my distress; be merciful to me and hear my prayer.
6:2 Be merciful to me, Lord, for I am faint; O Lord, heal me, for my bones are in agony. My soul is in anguish. How long, O Lord, how long?
25:6-7 Remember, O Lord, Your great mercy and love, for they are from of old. Remember not the sins of my youth and my rebellious ways; according to Your love remember me, for You are good, O Lord.
26:11 But I lead a blameless life; redeem me and be merciful to me.

30:8 To you, O Lord, I called; to the Lord I cried for mercy.
31:9-10 Be merciful to me, O Lord, for I am in distress; my eyes grow weak with sorrow, my soul and my body with grief. My life is consumed by anguish and my years by groaning; my strength fails because of my affliction, and my bones grow weak.
31:21 Praise be to the Lord, for He showed His wonderful love to me when I was in a besieged city.
40:11 Do not withhold Your mercy from me, O Lord; may Your love and Your truth always protect me.
51:1-2 Have mercy on me, O God, according to Your unfailing love; according to Your great compassion blot out my transgressions. Wash away all my iniquity and cleanse me from my sin.
57:1 Have mercy on me, O God, have mercy on me, for in You my soul takes refuge. I will take refuge in the shadow of Your wings until the disaster has passed.
69:16-17 Answer me, O Lord, out of the goodness of Your love; in Your great mercy turn to me. Do not hide Your face from Your servant; answer me quickly, for I am in trouble.
86:3 Have mercy on me, O Lord, for I call to You all day long.
86:6-7 Hear my prayer, O Lord; listen to my cry for mercy, in the day of my trouble I will call to You, for You will answer me.
86:16 Turn to me and have mercy on me; grant Your strength to Your servant
142:1-2 I cry aloud to the Lord; I lift up my voice to the Lord for mercy. I pour out my complaint before Him; before Him I tell my trouble.
143:1 O Lord, hear my prayer, listen to my cry for mercy; in Your faithfulness and righteousness come to my relief.

God shepherds you

28:8-9 The Lord is the strength of His people, a fortress of salvation for His anointed one. Save Your people and bless Your inheritance; be their shepherd and carry them forever.
95:6-7 Come, let us bow down in worship, let us kneel before the Lord our Maker; for He is our God and we are the people of His pasture, the flock under his care.
100:3 Know that the Lord is God. It is He who made us, and we are His; we are His people, the sheep of His pasture.

God is with you

14:5b God is present in the company of the righteous.
23:4 Even though I walk through the valley of the shadow of death, I will fear no evil, for You are with me; Your rod and Your staff, they comfort me.
31:7 I will be glad and rejoice in Your love, for You saw my affliction and knew the anguish of my soul.
46:7 The Lord Almighty is with us; the God of Jacob is our fortress.
73:23 Yet I am always with You; You hold me by my right hand.
91:14-16 "Because he loves me", says the Lord, "I will rescue him; I will protect him, for he acknowledges My name. He will call upon Me, and I will answer

him; I will be with him in trouble, I will deliver him and honor him. With long life will I satisfy him and show him My salvation.

139:7-11 Where can I go from Your Spirit? Where can I flee from Your presence? If I go up to the heavens, You are there; if I make my bed in the depths, You are there. If I rise on the wings of the dawn, if I settle on the far side of the sea, even there Your hand will guide me, Your right hand will hold me fast. If I say, "Surely the darkness will hide me and the light become night around me," even the darkness will not be dark to You; the night will shine like the day, for darkness is as light to You.

God is faithful to you

21:2 God, You have granted me the desire of my heart and have not withheld the request of my lips.

25:10 All the ways of the Lord are loving and faithful for those who keep the demands of His covenant.

36:5-6 Your love, O Lord, reaches to the heavens, Your faithfulness to the skies. Your righteousness is like the mighty mountains, Your justice like the great deep.

40:10 I do not hide Your righteousness in my heart; I speak of Your faithfulness and salvation. I do not conceal Your love and Your truth from the great assembly.

41:12 In my integrity You uphold me and set me in Your presence forever.

57:10 For great is Your love, reaching to the heavens; Your faithfulness reaches to the skies.

61:7 May I (David) be enthroned in God's presence forever; appoint Your love and faithfulness to protect me.

71:22 I will praise you with the harp for Your faithfulness, O my God; I will sing praise to You with the lyre

86:15 But you, O Lord, are a compassionate and gracious God, slow to anger, abounding in love and faithfulness.

89:1-2 I will sing of the Lord's great love forever; with my mouth I will make Your faithfulness known through all generation. I will declare that Your love stands firm forever, that You established Your faithfulness in heaven itself.

89:5 The heavens praise Your wonders, O Lord, Your faithfulness too, in the assembly of the holy ones.

89:14 Righteousness and justice are the foundation of Your throne; love and faithfulness go before You.

91:4 He will cover you with his feathers, and under His wings you will find refuge; His faithfulness will be your shield and rampart.

92:1-3 It is good to praise the Lord and make music to Your name, O Most High, to proclaim Your love in the morning and Your faithfulness at night, to the music of the ten-stringed lyre and the melody of the harp.

98:3 He has remembered His love and His faithfulness to the house of Israel; all the ends of the earth have seen the salvation of our God.

108:4 For great is Your love, higher than the heavens; Your faithfulness reaches to the skies.

115:1 Not to us, O Lord, not to us but to Your name be the glory, because of Your love and faithfulness.

143:1 O Lord, hear my prayer, listen to my cry for mercy; in Your faithfulness and righteousness come to my relief.

145:13b The Lord is faithful to all His promises and loving toward all He has made.

146:5-6 Blessed is the person whose help is God and whose hope is in the Lord their God, the Maker of heaven and earth, the sea, and everything in them— The Lord, who remains faithful forever.

God loves you

David describes God's love as unfailing, great, priceless, redeeming, enduring, protective, better than life, abounding, wonderful, supportive, forever, and worth singing about.

6:4 Turn, O Lord, and deliver me; save me because of Your unfailing love.

13:5 But I trust in Your unfailing love; my heart rejoices in Your salvation.

17:7 Show the wonder of Your great love, You who save by Your right hand those who take refuge in You from their foes.

25:6-7 Remember, O Lord, Your great mercy and love, for they are from of old. Remember not the sins of my youth and my rebellious ways; according to Your love remember me, for You are good, O Lord.

25:10 All the ways of the Lord are loving and faithful for those who keep the demands of His covenant.

26:3 For Your love, God, is ever before me, and I walk continually in Your truth.

31:7 I will be glad and rejoice in Your love, for You saw my affliction and knew the anguish of my soul.

33:18-19 But the eyes of the Lord are on those who fear Him, on those whose hope is in His unfailing love, to deliver them from death and keep them alive in famine.

33:22 May Your unfailing love rest upon us, O Lord, even as we put our hope in You.

36:5-6 Your love, O Lord, reaches to the heavens, Your faithfulness to the skies. Your righteousness is like the mighty mountains, Your justice like the great deep.

36:7-8 How priceless is Your unfailing love! Both high and low among men find refuge in the shadow of Your wings.

36:10 Continue Your love to those who know You, Your righteousness to the upright in heart.

40:10 I do not hide Your righteousness in my heart; I speak of Your faithfulness and salvation. I do not conceal Your love and Your truth from the great assembly.

40:11 Do not withhold Your mercy from me, O Lord; may Your love and Your truth always protect me.

44:26 Rise up and help us; redeem us because of Your unfailing love.

51:1-2 Have mercy on me, O God, according to Your unfailing love; according to Your great compassion blot out my transgressions. Wash away all my iniquity and cleanse me from my sin.

52:8 But I am like an olive tree flourishing in the house of God; I trust in God's unfailing love for ever and ever.

57:10 For great is Your love, reaching to the heavens; Your faithfulness reaches to the skies.

59:16-17 I will sing of Your (God's) strength, in the morning I will sing of Your love; for You are my fortress, my refuge in times of trouble. O my Strength, I sing praise to You; You, O God, are my fortress, my loving God.

61:7 May I (David) be enthroned in God's presence forever; appoint Your love and faithfulness to protect me.

62:11 One thing God has spoken, two things have I heard: that You, O God, are strong, and that You, O Lord, are loving.

63:3 Because Your (God) love is better than life, my lips will glorify You.

66:20 Praise be to God, who has not rejected my prayer or withheld His love from me!

69:13 But I pray to You, O Lord, in the time of Your favor; in Your great love, O God, answer me with Your sure salvation.

69:16-17 Answer me, O Lord, out of the goodness of Your love; in Your great mercy turn to me. Do not hide Your face from Your servant; answer me quickly, for I am in trouble.

85:7 Show us Your unfailing love, O Lord, and grant us Your salvation.

86:5 You are forgiving and good, O Lord, abounding in love to all who call to You.

86:13 For great is Your love toward me; You have delivered me from the depths of the grave.

86:15 But you, O Lord, are a compassionate and gracious God, slow to anger, abounding in love and faithfulness.

89:1-2 I will sing of the Lord's great love forever; with my mouth I will make Your faithfulness known through all generation. I will declare that Your love stands firm forever, that You established Your faithfulness in heaven itself.

89:14 Righteousness and justice are the foundation of Your throne; love and faithfulness go before You.

90:14 Satisfy us in the morning with Your unfailing love, that we may sing for joy and be glad all our days.

92:1-3 It is good to praise the Lord and make music to Your name, O Most High, to proclaim Your love in the morning and Your faithfulness at night, to the music of the ten-stringed lyre and the melody of the harp.

94:18 When I said, "My foot is slipping," Your love, O Lord, supported me.

98:3 He has remembered His love and His faithfulness to the house of Israel; all the ends of the earth have seen the salvation of our God.

100:5 For the Lord is good and His love endures forever; His faithfulness continues through all generations.

101:1 I will sing of Your love and justice; to you, O Lord, I will sing praise.

103:3-4 God forgives all your sins and heals all your disease, who redeems Your life from the pit and crowns you with love and compassion.

103:8 the Lord is compassionate and gracious, slow to anger, abounding in love.

103:11 For as high as the heavens are above the earth, so great is His love for those who fear Him.

103:17 But from everlasting to everlasting the Lord's love is with those who fear Him, and His righteousness with their children's children- with those who keep His covenant and remember to obey His precepts.

106:1, 107:1 Give thanks to the Lord, for He is good; His love endures forever.

107:8-9 Let them give thanks to the Lord for His unfailing love and His wonderful deeds for men, for He satisfies the thirsty and fills the hungry with good things.

107:43 Whoever is wise, let him heed these things (miracles that God performs in **107:33-42**) and consider the great love of the Lord.

108:4 For great is Your love, higher than the heavens; Your faithfulness reaches to the skies.

108:6 Save us and help us with Your right hand, that those You love may be delivered.

108:26 Help me, O Lord my God; save me in accordance with Your love.

115:1 Not to us, O Lord, not to us but to Your name be the glory, because of Your love and faithfulness.

119:41 May Your unfailing love come to me, O Lord, Your salvation according to Your promise

119:64 The earth is filled with Your love, O Lord; teach me Your decrees.

119:76 May Your unfailing love be my comfort, according to Your promise to your servant.

138:8 The Lord will fulfill His purpose for me: Your love, O Lord, endures forever—do not abandon the works of Your hands.

143:8 Let the morning bring me word of Your unfailing love, for I have put my trust in You. Show me the way I should go, for to You I lift up my soul.

143:12 In Your unfailing love, silence my enemies

144:2 He is my loving God and my fortress, my stronghold and my deliverer, my shield, in Whom I take refuge.

145:8 The Lord is gracious and compassionate, slow to anger and rich in love.

145:13b The Lord is faithful to all His promises and loving toward all He has made.

145:17 The Lord is righteous in all His ways and loving toward all He has made.

146:8 The Lord gives sight to the blind, the Lord lifts up those who are bowed down, the Lord loves the righteous.

147:11 The Lord delights in those who fear Him, who put their hope in His unfailing love.

God gives you peace

4:8 I will lie down and sleep in peace, for You alone, O Lord, make me dwell in safety.

23:2 He makes me lie down in green pastures, He leads me beside quiet waters, He restores my soul.

37:11 But the meek will inherit the land and enjoy great peace.

46:10 Be still and know that I am God; I will be exalted among the nations, I will be exalted in the earth.

85:8 I will listen to what God the Lord will say; He promises peace to His people

GOD IS YOUR STRONGHOLD:

God sustains you

3:5 I lie down and sleep; I wake again, because the Lord sustains me.
18:35 You give me Your shield of victory, and Your right hand sustains me; You stoop down to make me great.
51:10-12 Create in me a pure heart, O God, and renew a steadfast spirit within me. Do not cast me from Your presence or take Your Holy Spirit from me. Restore to me the joy of Your salvation and grant me a willing spirit, to sustain me.
54:4 Surely God is my help; the Lord is the one who sustains me.
55:22 Cast Your cares on the Lord and He will sustain you; He will never let the righteous fall.
146:9 The Lord watches over the alien and sustains the fatherless and the widow, but He frustrates the ways of the wicked.
147:6 The Lord sustains the humble but casts the wicked to the ground

God supports and guards you

86:2 Guard my life, for I am devoted to You. You are my God; save Your servant who trusts in You.
91:11-13 For He will command his angels concerning you to guard you in all your ways; they will lift you up in their hands, so that you will not strike your foot against a stone. You will tread upon the lion and the cobra; you will trample the great lion and the serpent.
94:18 When I said, "My foot is slipping," Your love, O Lord, supported me.
97:10 Let those who love the Lord hate evil, for He guards the lives of His faithful ones and delivers them from the hand of the wicked.

God is your Rock

18:31-32a For who is God besides the Lord? And who is the Rock except our God? It is God who arms me with strength
18:46, 49 The Lord lives! Praise be to my Rock! Exalted be God my Savior! I will praise you among the nations, O Lord; I will sing praises to Your name.
19:14 May the words of my mouth and the meditation of my heart be pleasing in Your sight, O Lord, my Rock and my Redeemer.
27:5 For the day of trouble He will keep me safe in His dwelling; He will hide me in the shelter of His tabernacle and set me high upon a rock.
28:1 To you I call, O Lord my Rock; do not turn a deaf ear to me. For if You remain silent, I will be like those who have gone down to the pit.
31:2-3 Turn Your ear to me, come quickly to my rescue; by my rock of refuge, a strong fortress to save me. Since You are my rock and my fortress, for the sake of Your name lead and guide me.
62:7 My salvation and my honor depend on God; He is my mighty rock, my refuge.

71:3 Be my Rock of refuge, to which I can always go; give the command to save me.

94:22 But the Lord has become my fortress, and my God the Rock in whom I take refuge.

95:1-2 Come, let us sing for joy to the Lord; let us shout aloud to the Rock of our salvation. Let us come before Him with thanksgiving and extol Him with music and song.

144:1 Praise be to the Lord my Rock, who trains my hands for wary, my finger for battle.

God is your shield

84:11 For the Lord God is a sun and shield; the Lord bestows favor and honor; no good thing does He withhold from those whose walk is blameless.

115:11 You who fear Him, trust in the Lord—He is their help and shield.

119:114 You are my refuge and my shield; I have put my hope in Your word.

143:9 Rescue me from my enemies, O Lord, for I hide myself in You.

144:2 He is my loving God and my fortress, my stronghold and my deliverer, my shield, in whom I take refuge.

God is strong and powerful

18:39-40 God armed me with strength for battle; You made my adversaries bow at my feet. You made my enemies turn their backs in flight, and I destroyed my foes.

24:7,10 Who is this King of glory? The Lord strong and mighty, the Lord might in battle.

27:1 The Lord is my light and my salvation—whom shall I fear? The Lord is the stronghold of my life—of whom shall I be afraid?

29:3, 4, 5, 7, 8 9, 10 The voice of the Lord is over the waters; the God of glory thunders, the Lord thunders over the mighty waters. The voice of the Lord is powerful. The voice of the Lord breaks the cedars of Lebanon. The voice of the Lord strikes with flashes of lightning. The voice of the Lord shakes the desert. The voice of the Lord twists the oaks and strips the forests bare. The Lord sits enthroned over the flood; the Lord is enthroned as King forever.

46:1 God is our refuge and strength, an ever-present help in trouble.

59:16-17 I will sing of your (God's) strength, in the morning I will sing of Your love; for you are my fortress, my refuge in times of trouble. O my Strength, I sing praise to You; You, O God, are my fortress, my loving God.

62:2, 6 God alone is my Rock and my salvation; He is my fortress, I will never be shaken.

62:11 One thing God has spoken, two things have I heard: that You, O God, are strong, and that You, O Lord, are loving.

71:18 Even when I am old and gray, do not forsake me, O God, till I declare Your power to the next generation, Your might to all who are to come.

73:26 My flesh and my heart may fail, but God is the strength of my heart and my portion forever.

77:14 You are the God who performs miracles; You display Your power among the peoples.

86:16 Turn to me and have mercy on me; grant Your strength to Your servant
89:13 God's arm is endued with power; His hand is strong, His right hand exalted.
89:17 For God is our glory and strength
96:5-6 For all the gods of the nations are idols, but the Lord made the heavens. Splendor and majesty are before Him; strength and glory are in His sanctuary.
105:4 Look to the Lord and His strength; seek His face always.
106:6, 8 We have sinned, even as our fathers did; we have done wrong and acted wickedly. Yet God saves us for His names' sake, to make His mighty power known.
119:28 My soul is weary with sorrow; strengthen me according to Your word.
144:2 He is my loving God and my fortress, my stronghold and my deliverer, my shield, in whom I take refuge.
145:6 People will tell of the power of Your awesome works, and I will proclaim Your great deeds.

God watches over you

121:1-3 I lift up my eyes to the hills—where does my help come from? My help comes from the Lord, the Maker of heaven and earth. He will not let your foot slip—He who watches over you will not slumber
121:7-8 The Lord will keep you from all harm—He will watch over your life; the Lord will watch over your coming and going both now and forevermore.
145:20 The Lord watches over all who love Him
146:9 The Lord watches over the alien and sustains the fatherless and the widow, but He frustrates the ways of the wicked.

God rescues you

18:16-17, 19 God reached down from on high and took hold of me; He drew me out of deep waters. He rescued me from my powerful enemy, from my foes, who were too strong for me. He brought me out into a spacious place; He rescued me *because* He delighted in me.
25:20 Guard my life and rescue me; let me not be put to shame, for I take refuge in You.
30:1-3 I will exalt you, O Lord, for You lifted me out of the depths and did not let my enemies gloat over me. O Lord my God, I called to You for help and You healed me. O Lord, You brought me up from the grave; You spared me from going down into the pit.
31:2-3 Turn Your ear to me, come quickly to my rescue; by my Rock of refuge, a strong fortress to save me. Since You are my Rock and my fortress, for the sake of Your name lead and guide me.
40:2 God lifted me out of the slimy pit, out of the mud and mire; He set my feet on a rock and gave me a firm place to stand.
69:14 Rescue me (O God) from the mire, do not let me sink
71:2 Rescue me and deliver me in Your righteousness; turn Your ear to me and save me.
81:7 In your distress you called and I rescued you, I answered you out of a thundercloud-

91:14-16 "Because he loves me", says the Lord, "I will rescue him; I will protect him, for he acknowledges My name. He will call upon Me, and I will answer him; I will be with him in trouble, I will deliver him and honor him. With long life will I satisfy him and show him My salvation.
140:1 Rescue me, O Lord, from evil people; protect me from men of violence
142:6 Listen to my cry, for I am in desperate need; rescue me from those who pursue me, for they are too strong for me.
143:9 Rescue me from my enemies, O Lord, for I hide myself in You.
144:7 Reach down Your hand from on high; deliver me and rescue me from the mighty waters

God delivers you from difficulties

3:8 From the Lord comes deliverance from my enemies
6:4 Turn, O Lord, and deliver me; save me because of Your unfailing love.
7:1 O Lord God, I take refuge in You; save and deliver me from all who pursue me, or they will tear me like a lion.
18:29 With God's help I can advance against a troop; with my God I can scale a wall.
22:6, 8 But I am a worm and not a man, scorned by men and despised by the people. He trusts in the Lord; let the Lord rescue him. Let Him deliver him, since he delights in Him.
25:15 My eyes are ever on the Lord, for only He will release my feet from the snare.
31:1 In you, O Lord, I have taken refuge; let me never be put to shame; deliver me in Your righteousness.
32:7 You are my hiding place; You will protect me from trouble and surround me with songs of deliverance.
33:18-19 But the eyes of the Lord are on those who fear Him, on those whose hope is in His unfailing love, to deliver them from death and keep them alive in famine.
34:4 I sought the Lord, and He answered me; He delivered me from all my fears. The angel of the Lord encamps around those who fear Him, and He delivers them.
40:17 Yet I am poor and needy; may the Lord think of me. You are my help and my deliverer; O my God, do not delay.
50:15 God says, "Call upon Me in the day of trouble; I will deliver you, and you will honor Me."
54:7 For God has delivered me from all my troubles, and my eyes have looked in triumph on my foes.
56:13 For You (God) have delivered me from death and my feet from stumbling, that I may walk before God in the light of life.
70:5 Yet I am poor and needy; come quickly to me, O God. You are my help and my deliverer; O Lord, do not delay.
71:2 Rescue me and deliver me in Your righteousness; turn Your ear to me and save me.
72:12-13 God will deliver the needy who cry out, the afflicted who have no one to help. He will take pity on the weak and the needy and save the needy from death.

86:13 For great is Your love toward me; You have delivered me from the depths of the grave.

91:14-16 "Because he loves me", says the Lord, "I will rescue him; I will protect him, for he acknowledges my name. He will call upon me, and I will answer him; I will be with him in trouble, I will deliver him and honor him. With long life will I satisfy him and show him my salvation.

97:10 Let those who love the Lord hate evil, for He guards the lives of His faithful ones and delivers them from the hand of the wicked.

107:5-6 They were hungry and thirsty, and their lives ebbed away. Then they cried out to the Lord in their trouble, and He delivered them from their distress.

107:14 He brought them out of darkness and the deepest gloom and broke away their chains.

108:6 Save us and help us with Your right hand, that those You love may be delivered.

109:21-22 But You, O Sovereign Lord, deal well with me for Your name's sake; out of the goodness of Your love, deliver me. For I am poor and needy, and my heart is wounded within me.

116:8 For You, O Lord, have delivered my soul from death, my eyes from tears, my feet from stumbling, that I may walk before the Lord

119:153 Look upon my suffering and deliver me, for I have not forgotten Your law.

144:2 He is my loving God and my fortress, my stronghold and my deliverer, my shield, in whom I take refuge.

144:7 Reach down Your hand from on high; deliver me and rescue me from the mighty waters

God is your refuge

2:12b Blessed are all who take refuge in the Lord.

5:11 But let all who take refuge in You be glad; let them ever sing for joy. Spread Your protection over them, that those who love Your name may rejoice in You. **5:12** For surely, O Lord, You bless the righteous; You surround them with Your favor as with a shield.

7:1 O Lord God, I take refuge in You; save and deliver me from all who pursue me, or they will tear me like a lion.

11:1 In the Lord I take refuge. How then can my enemies say to me: "Flee like a bird to your mountain."

16:1 Keep me safe, O God, for in You I take refuge.

17:7 Show the wonder of Your great love, You who save by Your right hand those who take refuge in You from their foes.

18:2 The Lord is my Rock, my fortress and my deliverer; my God is my Rock, in whom I take refuge. His is my shield and the horn of my salvation, my stronghold.

18:30b God is a shield for all who take refuge in Him.

25:20 Guard my life and rescue me; let me not be put to shame, for I take refuge in You.

31:1 In You, O Lord, I have taken refuge; let me never be put to shame; deliver me in Your righteousness.

31:19 How great is Your goodness, which You have stored up for those who fear You, which You bestow in the sight of men on those who take refuge in You.

34:8 Taste and see that the Lord is good; blessed is the man who takes refuge in Him.

36:7-8 How priceless is Your unfailing love! Both high and low among men find refuge in the shadow of Your wings.

46:1 God is our refuge and strength, an ever-present help in trouble.

57:1 Have mercy on me, O God, have mercy on me, for in You my soul takes refuge. I will take refuge in the shadow of Your wings until the disaster has passed.

61:2-3 For the ends of the earth I call to You, I call as my heart grows faint; lead me to the Rock that is higher than I. For You have been my refuge, as strong tower against the foe.

61:4 I long to dwell in Your tent forever and take refuge in the shelter of Your wings.

62:7 My salvation and my honor depend on God; He is my might rock, my refuge.

62:8 Trust in God all times, O people; pour out your hearts to Him, for God is our refuge.

64:10 Let the righteous rejoice in the Lord and take refuge in Him; let all the upright in heart praise Him.

71:3 Be my Rock of refuge, to which I can always go; give the command to save me.

73:28 But as for me, it is good to be near God. I have made the Sovereign Lord my refuge; I will tell of all Your deeds.

91:2 I will say of the Lord, "He is my refuge and my fortress, my God, in whom I trust."

91:4 He will cover you with his feathers, and under His wings you will find refuge; his faithfulness will be your shield and rampart.

91:9-10 If you make the Most High your dwelling- even the Lord, who is my refuge- then no harm will befall you, no disaster will come near your tent.

94:22 But the Lord has become my fortress, and my God the rock in whom I take refuge.

118:8 It is better to take refuge in the Lord than to trust in man.

119:114 You are my refuge and my shield; I have put my hope in Your word.

141:8 But my eyes are fixed on you, O Sovereign Lord; in You I take refuge—do not give me over to death.

142:5 I cry to you, O Lord; I say "you are my refuge, my portion in the land of the living."

144:2 He is my loving God and my fortress, my stronghold and my deliverer, my shield, in whom I take refuge.

God helps you

18:35 You give me Your shield of victory, and Your right hand sustains me; You stoop down to make me great.

40:13 Be pleased, O Lord, to save me; O Lord, come quickly to help me.

40:17 Yet I am poor and needy; may the Lord think of me. You are my help and my deliverer; O my God, do not delay.

44:26 Rise up and help us; redeem us because of Your unfailing love.

54:4 Surely God is my help; the Lord is the one who sustains me.

60:11-12 Give us aid against the enemy, for the help of man is worthless. With God we will gain the victory, and He will trample down our enemies.

63:7 Because You are my help, I sing in the shadow of Your wings.

69:1-3 Save me, O God, for the waters have come up to my neck. I sink in the miry depths, where there is no foothold. I have come into the deep waters; the floods engulf me. I am worn out calling for help; my throat is parched. My eyes fail, looking for my God.

70:1 Hasten, O God, to save me; O Lord, come quickly to help me.

70:5 Yet I am poor and needy; come quickly to me, O God. You are my help and my deliverer; O Lord, do not delay.

71:12 Be not far from me, O God; come quickly, O my God, to help me.

77:1 I cried out to God for help; I cried out to God to hear me.

86:17 Give me a sign of Your goodness, that my enemies may see it and be put to shame, for You, O Lord, have helped me and comforted me.

94:17 Unless the Lord had given me help, I would soon have dwelt in the silence of death.

107:8-9 Let them give thanks to the Lord for His unfailing love and His wonderful deeds for men, for He satisfies the thirsty and fills the hungry with good things.

108:6 Save us and help us with Your right hand, that those you love may be delivered.

108:12-13 Give us aid against the enemy, for the help of man is worthless. With God we will gain the victory, and He will trample down our enemies.

115:11 You who fear Him, trust in the Lord—He is their help and shield.

121:1-3 I lift up my eyes to the hills—where does my help come from? My help comes from the Lord, the Maker of heaven and earth. He will not let your foot slip—He who watches over you will not slumber

124:8 Our help is in the name of the Lord, the Maker of heaven and earth.

145:4 The Lord upholds all those who fall and lifts up all who are bowed down.

146:5-6 Blessed is the person whose help is God and whose hope is in the Lord their God, the Maker of heaven and earth, the sea, and everything in them—The Lord, who remains faithful forever.

146:8 The Lord gives sight to the blind, the Lord lifts up those who are bowed down, the Lord loves the righteous.

God is your protector

3:3 But You are a shield around me, O Lord; You bestow glory on me and lift up my head. (this is especially true when we think we are surrounded by so many obstacles in life)

5:11-12 But let all who take refuge in You be glad; let them every sing for joy. Spread Your protection over them, that those who love Your name may rejoice in You. For surely, O Lord, You bless the righteous; You surround them with Your favor as with a shield.

7:10 My shield is God Most High, who saves the upright in heart.

12:5-6 Because of the oppression of the weak and the groaning of the needy, I will now arise," says the Lord. "I will protect them from those who malign them."

17:8 Lord, hide me in the shadow of Your wings from the wicked who assail me

18:30b God is a shield for all who take refuge in Him.

18:35 You give me Your shield of victory, and Your right hand sustains me; You stoop down to make me great.

20:1 May the Lord answer you when you are in distress; may the name of the God of Jacob protect you.

23:5 You prepare a table before me in the presence of my enemies. You anoint my head with oil; my cup overflows.

25:20 Guard my life and rescue me; let me not be put to shame, for I take refuge in You.

27:5 For the day of trouble He will keep me safe in his dwelling; He will hide me in the shelter of his tabernacle and set me high upon a rock.

28:7 The Lord is my strength and my shield; my heart trusts in Him, and I am helped. My heart leaps for joy and I will give thanks to Him in song.

32:7 You are my hiding place; You will protect me from trouble and surround me with songs of deliverance.

33:20 We wait in hope for the Lord; He is our help and our shield.

40:11 Do not withhold Your mercy from me, O Lord; may Your love and Your truth always protect me.

59:16-17 I will sing of Your (God's) strength, in the morning I will sing of Your love; for You are my fortress, my refuge in times of trouble. O my Strength, I sing praise to You; You, O God, are my fortress, my loving God.

62:7 My salvation and my honor depend on God; He is my might rock, my refuge.

64:1 Hear me, O God, as I voice my complaint; protect my life from the threat of the enemy.

69:29 I am in pain and distress; may Your salvation, O God, protect me.

89:18 Indeed, our shield belongs to the Lord, our king to the Holy One of Israel.

91:14-16 "Because He loves me", says the Lord, "I will rescue him; I will protect him, for he acknowledges my name. He will call upon Me, and I will answer him; I will be with him in trouble, I will deliver him and honor him. With long life will I satisfy him and show him My salvation.

116:6 The Lord protects the simplehearted; when I was in great need, He saved me.

140:1 Rescue me, O Lord, from evil people; protect me from men of violence

140:4 Keep me, O Lord, from the hands of the wicked; protect me from people of violence who plan to trip my feet

God is your security

4:8 I will lie down and sleep in peace, for You alone, O Lord, make me dwell in safety.

16:5a Lord, You have assigned me my portion and my cup You have made my lot secure.

16:6 I have set the Lord always before me. Because He is at my right hand, I will not be shaken.

16:9-10 Therefore my heart is glad (because I have set the Lord always before me and therefore I am not shaken) and my tongue rejoices; my body also will rest secure, because You will not abandon me to the grave, nor will You let your Holy One see decay.

17:14 O Lord, by Your hand save me from such men, from men of this world whose reward is in this life.

18:31-32a For who is God besides the Lord? And who is the Rock except our God? It is God who arms me with strength

18:36 God broadens the path beneath me, so that my ankles do not turn.

27:5 For the day of trouble He will keep me safe in His dwelling; He will hide me in the shelter of His tabernacle and set me high upon a rock.

59:16-17 I will sing of Your (God's) strength, in the morning I will sing of Your love; for You are my fortress, my refuge in times of trouble. O my Strength, I sing praise to You; You, O God, are my fortress, my loving God.

66:8-9 Praise our God, O people, let the sound of His praise be heard; He has preserved our lives and kept our feet from slipping.

112:8 His heart is secure, He will have no fear; in the end He will look in triumph on His foes.

119:25 I am laid low in the dust; preserve my life according to Your word.

119:50 My comfort in my suffering is this; Your promise preserves my life.

119:156 Your compassion is great, O Lord; preserve my life according to Your laws.

138:7 Though I walk in the middle of trouble, You preserve my life

143:11 For Your name's sake, O Lord, preserve my life; in Your righteousness, bring me out of trouble.

GOD WANTS A RELATIONSHIP WITH YOU:

God answers you when you pray

4:1 Answer me when I call to you, O my righteous God, give me relief from my distress; be merciful to me and hear my prayer.

20:1 May the Lord answer you when you are in distress; may the name of the God of Jacob protect you.

20:4 May God give you the desire of your heart and make all your plans succeed.

20:6 Now I know that the Lord saves His anointed; He answers him from His holy heaven with the saving power of His right hand.

27:14 Wait for the Lord; be strong and take heart and wait for the Lord.

28:1 To you I call, O Lord my Rock; do not turn a deaf ear to me. For if You remain silent, I will be like those who have gone down to the pit.

34:4 I sought the Lord, and He answered me; He delivered me from all my fears. The angel of the Lord encamps around those who fear Him, and He delivers them.

38:15, 21, 22 I wait for you, O Lord; You will answer, O Lord my God. O Lord, do not forsake me; be not far from me, O my God. Come quickly to help me, O Lord my Savior.

65:5 You answer us with awesome deeds of righteousness, O God our Savior, the hope of all the ends of the earth and of the farthest seas

69:16-17 Answer me, O Lord, out of the goodness of Your love; in Your great mercy turn to me. Do not hide Your face from Your servant; answer me quickly, for I am in trouble.

91:14-16 "Because he loves me", says the Lord, "I will rescue him; I will protect him, for he acknowledges My name. He will call upon Me, and I will answer him; I will be with him in trouble, I will deliver him and honor him. With long life will I satisfy him and show him My salvation.

99:6 Moses and Aaron were among His priests, Samuel as among those who called on His name; they called on the Lord and He answered them.

99:8 O Lord our God, You answered them; You were to Israel a forgiving God, though You punished their misdeeds.

102:2 Do not hide Your face from me when I am in distress. Turn Your ear to me; when I call, answer me quickly.

120:1 I call on the Lord in my distress, and He answers me.

138:3 When I called, You answered me; You made me bold and stouthearted.

143:7 Answer me quickly, O Lord; my spirit fails. Do not hide Your face from me or I will be like those who go down to the pit.

God listens to you

10:12, 17-18 Arise, Lord! Lift Your hand, O God. Do not forget the helpless. You hear, O Lord, the desire of the afflicted; You encourage them, and You listen to their cry, defending the fatherless and the oppressed, in order that man, who is of the earth, may terrify no more.

18:4-6 The cords of death entangled me; the torrents of destruction overwhelmed me. The cords of the grave coiled around me; the snares of death confronted me. In my distress I called to the Lord; I cried to my God for help. From His temple he heard my voice; my cry came before Him, into His ears.

20:9b Answer us when we call!

21:2 God, You have granted me the desire of my heart and have not withheld the request of my lips.

31:2-3 Turn Your ear to me, come quickly to my rescue; by my Rock of refuge, a strong fortress to save me. Since You are my Rock and my fortress, for the sake of Your name lead and guide me.

34:15 The eyes of the Lord are on the righteous and His ears are attentive to their cry.

39:12 "Hear my prayer, O Lord, listen to my cry for help; be not deaf to my weeping."

40:1 I waited patiently for the Lord; He turned to me and heard my cry.

54:1-2 Save me, O God, by Your name; vindicate me by Your might. Hear my prayer, O God; listen to the words of my mouth.

66:18-19 If I had cherished sin in my heart, the Lord would not have listened; but God has surely listened and heard my voice in prayer.

71:2 Rescue me and deliver me in Your righteousness; turn Your ear to me and save me.

84:8 Hear my prayer, O Lord God Almighty; listen to me, O God of Jacob.

86:1 Hear, O Lord, and answer me, for I am poor and needy.

God wants to show you grace

25:16 Turn to me and be gracious to me, for I am lonely and afflicted.
67:1 May God be gracious to us and bless us and make His face shine upon us.
86:15 But you, O Lord, are a compassionate and gracious God, slow to anger, abounding in love and faithfulness.
103:8 The Lord is compassionate and gracious, slow to anger, abounding in love.
111:4 He has caused His wonders to be remembered; the Lord is gracious and compassionate.
116:5 The Lord is gracious and righteous; our God is full of compassion.
145:8 The Lord is gracious and compassionate, slow to anger and rich in love.

GOD IS PREEMINENT IN THE WORLD:

God is Majestic

93:1 The Lord reigns, He is robed in majesty; the Lord is robed in majesty and is armed with strength.
96:5-6 For all the gods of the nations are idols, but the Lord made the heavens. Splendor and majesty are before Him; strength and glory are in His sanctuary.
111:3 Glorious and majestic are His deeds, and His righteousness endures forever.
145:5 People will speak of the glorious splendor of Your majesty, and I will meditate on Your wonderful works.

God is marvelous

96:3 Declare his glory among the nations, His marvelous deeds among all peoples.
96:5-6 For all the gods of the nations are idols, but the Lord made the heavens. Splendor and majesty are before Him; strength and glory are in His sanctuary.

God performs miracles and mighty acts

77:14 You are the God who performs miracles; You display your power among the peoples.
114:8 God turned the rock into a pool, the hard rock into springs of water.
145:4 One generation will commend Your works to another; they will tell of Your mighty acts.
145:11 People will tell of the glory of Your kingdom and speak of Your might, so that men may know of Your mighty acts and the glorious splendor of Your kingdom.

God is good

25:8 Good and upright is the Lord; therefor He instructs sinners in His ways.
31:19 How great is Your goodness, which You have stored up for those who fear You, which you bestow in the sight of men on those who take refuge in you.
86:5 You are forgiving and good, O Lord, abounding in love to all who call to You.
86:17 Give me a sign of Your goodness, that my enemies may see it and be put to shame, for You, O Lord, have helped me and comforted me.
106:1 Give thanks to the Lord, for He is good; His love endures forever.
109:21-22 But you, O Sovereign Lord, deal well with me for Your name's sake; out of the goodness of Your love, deliver me. For I am poor and needy, and my heart is wounded within me.
116:7 Be at rest once more, O my soul, for the Lord has been good to you.
116:12 How can I repay the Lord for all His goodness to me?
142:7 Set me free from my prison, that I may praise Your name. Then the righteous will gather about me because of Your goodness to me.
143:10 Teach me to do Your will, for You are my God; may Your good Spirit lead me on level ground.
145:7 People will celebrate Your abundant goodness and joyfully sing of Your righteousness.
145:9 The Lord is good to all; He has compassion on all He has made.

God is great

95:3-5 For the Lord is the great God, the great King above all gods. In His hand are the depths of the earth, and the mountain peaks belong to Him. The sea is His, for He made it, and His hands formed the dry land.
96:4 For great is the Lord and most worthy of praise; He is to be feared above all gods.
111:2 Great are the works of the Lord; they are pondered by all who delight in them.
135:5-7 I know that the Lord is great, that our Lord does whatever please Him, in the heavens and on the earth, in the seas and all their depths. He makes clouds rise from the ends of the earth; He sends lightning with the rain and brings out the wind from his storehouses.
145:3 Great is the Lord and most worthy of praise; His greatness no one can fathom.
145:6 People will tell of the power of Your awesome works, and I will proclaim Your great deeds.
147:5 Great is our Lord and mighty in power; His understanding has no limit.

God is forever/eternal

48:14 For this God is our God for ever and ever; He will be our guide even to the end.
93:2 Your throne was established long ago; You are from all eternity.

111:3 Glorious and majestic are His deeds, and His righteousness endures forever.

145:13 Your kingdom is an everlasting kingdom, and Your dominion endures through all generations.

God is full of glory

89:17 For God is our glory and strength

96:3 Declare His glory among the nations, His marvelous deeds among all peoples.

96:5-6 For all the gods of the nations are idols, but the Lord made the heavens. Splendor and majesty are before Him; strength and glory are in His sanctuary.

111:3 Glorious and majestic are His deeds, and His righteousness endures forever.

115:1 Not to us, O Lord, not to us but to Your name be the glory, because of Your love and faithfulness.

145:5 People will speak of the glorious splendor of Your majesty, and I will meditate on Your wonderful works.

145:11 People will tell of the glory of Your kingdom and speak of Your might, so that men may know of Your mighty acts and the glorious splendor of Your kingdom.

God is supreme

86:8-10 Among the gods there is none like You, O Lord; no deeds can compare with Yours. All the nations You have made will come and worship before You, O Lord; they will bring glory to Your name. For you are great and do marvelous deeds; You alone are God.

89:6 For who in the skies above can compare with the Lord? Who is like the Lord among the heavenly beings?

89:7b God is more awesome than all who surround Him.

89:8 O Lord God Almighty, who is like You? You are mighty, O Lord, and Your faithfulness surrounds You.

89:11 The heavens are Yours, and Yours also the earth; You founded the world and all that is in it.

95:3-5 For the Lord is the great God, the great King above all gods. In His hand are the depths of the earth, and the mountain peaks belong to Him. The sea is His, for He made it, and His hands formed the dry land.

96:5-6 For all the gods of the nations are idols, but the Lord made the heavens. Splendor and majesty are before Him; strength and glory are in His sanctuary.

97:7 All who worship images are put to shame, those who boast in idols—worship Him, all you gods!

97:9 For You, O Lord, are the most High over all the earth; You are exalted far above all gods.

113:5-6 Who is like the Lord our God, the One who sits enthroned on high, who stoops down to look on the heavens and the earth?

115:3 Our God is in heaven; He does whatever pleases Him.

God is full of wonders

9:1-2 I will praise you, O Lord, with all my heart; I will tell of all Your wonders. I will be glad and rejoice in You; I will sing praise to Your name, O Most High.
40:5 Many, O Lord my God, are the wonders You have done.
89:5 The heavens praise Your wonders, O Lord, Your faithfulness too, in the assembly of the holy ones.
111:4 He has caused His wonders to be remembered; the Lord is gracious and compassionate.

GOD RENEWS YOU:

God redeems you

19:14 May the words of my mouth and the meditation of my heart be pleasing in Your sight, O Lord, my Rock and my Redeemer.
25:22 Redeem Israel, O God, from all their troubles!
26:11 But I lead a blameless life; redeem me and be merciful to me.
31:5 Into Your hands I commit my spirit; redeem me, O Lord, the God of truth.
44:26 Rise up and help us; redeem us because of Your unfailing love.
49:15 But God will redeem my life from the grave; He will surely take me to Himself
71:23-24 My lips will shout for joy when I sing praise to You-I, whom you have redeemed. My tongue will tell of Your righteous acts all day long
77:15a With Your (God) mighty arm You redeemed Your people
103:3-4 God forgives all your sins and heals all your disease, who redeems your life from the pit and crowns you with love and compassion.
106:10 God saved His people from the hand of the foe; from the hand of the enemy He redeemed them.

God restores you

23:2 He makes me lie down in green pastures, He leads me beside quiet waters, He restores my soul.
71:20-21 Though You have made me see troubles, many and bitter, You will restore my life again; from the depths of the earth You will again bring me up. You will increase my honor and comfort me once again.
80:3, 7, 19 Restore us, O God; make Your face shine upon us, that we may be saved.
85:1 You showed favor to Your land, O Lord; You restored the fortunes of Jacob.
85:4 Restore us again, O God our Savior, and put away Your displeasure toward us.

God revives you

19:7a The law of the Lord is perfect, reviving the soul.
85:6 Will You (God) not revive us again, that Your people may rejoice in You?

God saves you

7:1 O Lord God, I take refuge in You; save and deliver me from all who pursue me, or they will tear me like a lion.
7:10 My shield is God Most High, who saves the upright in heart.
13:5 But I trust in Your unfailing love; my heart rejoices in Your salvation.
16:9-10 Therefore my heart is glad (because I have set the Lord always before me and therefore I am not shaken) and my tongue rejoices; my body also will rest secure, because You will not abandon me to the grave, nor will you let Your Holy One see decay.
17:7 Show the wonder of Your great love, You who save by Your right hand those who take refuge in You from their foes.
17:14 O Lord, by Your hand save me from such men, from men of this world whose reward is in this life.
17:15 And I—in righteousness I will see Your face; when I awake, I will be satisfied with seeing Your likeness.
18:2 The Lord is my Rock, my fortress and my deliverer; my God is my Rock, in whom I take refuge. His is my shield and the horn of my salvation, my stronghold.
20:6 Now I know that the Lord saves His anointed; He answers him from His holy heaven with the saving power of His right hand.
21:4 I asked You for life, and You gave it to me—length of days, for ever and ever.
21:6 Surely You have granted him eternal blessings and made him glad with the joy of Your presence.
25:4-5 Show me Your ways, O Lord, teach me Your paths; guide me in Your truth and teach me, for You are God my Savior, and my hope is in You all day long.
27:1 The Lord is my light and my salvation—whom shall I fear? The Lord is the stronghold of my life—of whom shall I be afraid?
28:8-9 The Lord is the strength of His people, a fortress of salvation for His anointed one. Save Your people and bless Your inheritance; be their shepherd and carry them forever.
30:1-3 I will exalt You, O Lord, for You lifted me out of the depths and did not let my enemies gloat over me. O Lord my God, I called to You for help and You healed me. O Lord, You brought me up from the grave; You spared me from going down into the pit.
31:2-3 Turn Your ear to me, come quickly to my rescue; by my Rock of refuge, a strong fortress to save me. Since You are my Rock and my fortress, for the sake of Your name lead and guide me.
31:16 Let Your face shine on Your servant; save me in Your unfailing love.
40:10 I do not hide Your righteousness in my heart; I speak of Your faithfulness and salvation. I do not conceal Your love and Your truth from the great assembly.

40:13 Be pleased, O Lord, to save me; O Lord, come quickly to help me.

51:10-12 Create in me a pure heart, O God, and renew a steadfast spirit within me. Do not cast me from Your presence or take Your Holy Spirit from me. Restore to me the joy of Your salvation and grant me a willing spirit, to sustain me.

54:1-2 Save me, O God, by Your name; vindicate me by Your might. Hear my prayer, O God; listen to the words of my mouth.

55:16-18 But I call to God, and the Lord saves me. Evening, morning and noon I cry out in distress, and He hears my voice. He ransoms me unharmed from the battle wages against me, even though they may oppose me.

60:5 Save us and help us with Your right hand, that those You love may be delivered.

62:1 My soul finds rest in God alone; my salvation come from Him.

62:2,6 God alone is my Rock and my salvation; He is my fortress, I will never be shaken.

62:7 My salvation and my honor depend on God; He is my might Rock, my refuge.

68:20 Our God is a God who saves; from the Sovereign Lord comes escape from death.

69:1-3 Save me, O God, for the waters have come up to my neck. I sink in the miry depths, where there is no foothold. I have come into the deep waters; the floods engulf me. I am worn out calling for help; my throat is parched. My eyes fail, looking for my God.

69:13 But I pray to You, O Lord, in the time of Your favor; in Your great love, O God, answer me with Your sure salvation.

69:29 I am in pain and distress; may Your salvation, O God, protect me.

70:1 Hasten, O God, to save me; O Lord, come quickly to help me.

71:2 Rescue me and deliver me in your righteousness; turn Your ear to me and save me.

71:3 Be my Rock of refuge, to which I can always go; give the command to save me, for You are my Rock and my fortress.

71:15 My mouth will tell of Your righteousness, of Your salvation all day long, though I know not its measure.

80:3, 7,19 Restore us, O God; make Your face shine upon us, that we may be saved.

85:7 Show us Your unfailing love, O Lord, and grant us Your salvation.

85:9 Surely His salvation is near those who fear Him, that His glory may dwell in our land.

86:2 Guard my life, for I am devoted to You. You are my God; save Your servant who trusts in You.

88:1-2 O Lord, the God who saves me, day and night I cry out before You. May my prayer come before You; turn Your ear to my cry.

91:14-16 "Because he loves me", says the Lord, "I will rescue him; I will protect him, for he acknowledges My name. He will call upon Me, and I will answer him; I will be with him in trouble, I will deliver him and honor him. With long life will I satisfy him and show him My salvation.

95:1-2 Come, let us sing for joy to the Lord; let us shout aloud to the Rock of our salvation. Let us come before Him with thanksgiving and extol Him with music and song.

96:1-2 Sing to the Lord a new song; sing to the Lord, all the earth. Sing to the Lord, praise His name; proclaim His salvation day after day.

98:2 The Lord has made His salvation known and revealed His righteousness to the nations.

98:3 He has remembered His love and His faithfulness to the house of Israel; all the ends of the earth have seen the salvation of our God.

106:6, 8 We have sinned, even as our fathers did; we have done wrong and acted wickedly. Yet God saves us for His names' sake, to make His mighty power known.

106:10 God saved His people from the hand of the foe; from the hand of the enemy He redeemed them.

107:20 He sent forth His word and healed them; He rescued them from the grave.

108:6 Save us and help us with Your right hand, that those You love may be delivered.

108:26 Help me, O Lord my God; save me in accordance with Your love.

109:31 For He stands at the right hand of the need one, to save His life from those who condemn Him.

116:6 The Lord protects the simplehearted; when I was in great need, He saved me.

118:25 O Lord, save us; O Lord, grant us success.

119:41 May Your unfailing love come to me, O Lord, Your salvation according to Your promise

119:123 My eyes fail, looking for Your salvation, looking for Your righteous promise.

145:19 God fulfills the desires of those who fear Him; He hears their cry and saves them.

149:4 For the Lord takes delight in His people; He crowns the humble with salvation.

God forgives you

19:12 God can discern our errors. He can forgive my hidden faults.

25:11 For the sake of Your name, O Lord, forgive my iniquity, though it is great.

25:16-18 Turn to me and be gracious to me, for I am lonely and afflicted. The troubles of my heart have multiplied; free me from my anguish. Look upon my affliction and my distress and take away all my sins.

32: 1-2 Blessed is the person whose transgressions are forgiven, whose sins are covered, and whose sin the Lord does not count against him and in whose spirit is no deceit.

32:5 I acknowledged my sin to You and did not cover up my iniquity. I said, "I will confess my transgressions to the Lord"- and You forgave the guilt of my sin.

51:1-2 Have mercy on me, O God, according to Your unfailing love; according to Your great compassion blot out my transgressions. Wash away all my iniquity and cleanse me from my sin.

65:3 When we were overwhelmed by sins, You forgave our transgressions.

85:2 You (God) forgave the iniquity of Your people and covered all their sins.

86:5 You are forgiving and good, O Lord, abounding in love to all who call to You.

99:8 O Lord our God, You answered them; You were to Israel a forgiving God, though You punished their misdeeds.

103:3-4 God forgives all your sins and heals all your disease, who redeems your life from the pit and crowns you with love and compassion.

103:12 As far as the east is from the west, so far has He removed our transgressions from us.

130:3-4 If you, O Lord, kept a record of sins, O Lord, who could stand? But with You there is forgiveness; therefore You are feared.

GOD IS CREATOR, JUST AND RIGHTEOUS:

God controls everything

73:28 But as for me, it is good to be near God. I have made the Sovereign Lord my refuge; I will tell of all Your deeds.

107:29 He stilled the storm with a whisper; the waves of the sea were hushed.

109:21-22 But You, O Sovereign Lord, deal well with me for Your name's sake; out of the goodness of Your love, deliver me. For I am poor and needy, and my heart is wounded within me.

135:5-7 I know that the Lord is great, that our Lord does whatever pleases Him, in the heavens and on the earth, in the seas and all their depths. He makes clouds rise from the ends of the earth; He sends lightning with the rain and brings out the wind from his storehouses.

141:8 But my eyes are fixed on You, O Sovereign Lord; in You I take refuge—do not give me over to death.

God is the Creator

89:11 The heavens are Yours, and Yours also the earth; You founded the world and all that is in it.

89:12 You created the north and the south

95:3-5 For the Lord is the great God, the great King above all god. In His hand are the depths of the earth, and the mountain peaks belong to Him. The sea is His, for He made it, and His hands formed the dry land.

95:6-7 Come, let us bow down in worship, let us kneel before the Lord our Maker; for He is our God and we are the people of His pasture, the flock under His care.

96:5-6 For all the gods of the nations are idols, but the Lord made the heavens. Splendor and majesty are before Him; strength and glory are in His sanctuary.

100:3 Know that the Lord is God. It is He who made us, and we are His; we are His people, the sheep of His pasture.

118:24 This is the day that the Lord has made; let us rejoice and be glad in it.

121:1-3 I lift up my eyes to the hills—where does my help come from? My help comes from the Lord, the Maker of heaven and earth. He will not let your foot slip—He who watches over you will not slumber
124:8 Our help is in the name of the Lord, the Maker of heaven and earth.
145:9 The Lord is good to all; He has compassion on all He has made.
145:13b The Lord is faithful to all His promises and loving toward all He has made.
145:17 The Lord is righteous in all His ways and loving toward all He has made.
146:5-6 Blessed is the person whose help is God and whose hope is in the Lord their God, the Maker of heaven and earth, the sea, and everything in them—The Lord, who remains faithful forever.

God is truth

12:6 The words of the Lord are flawless, like silver refined in a furnace of clay, purified seven times.
31:5 Into your hands I commit my spirit; redeem me, O Lord, the God of truth.

God is just

26:1 Vindicate me, O Lord, for I have led a blameless life; I have trusted in the Lord without wavering.
54:1-2 Save me, O God, by Your name; vindicate me by Your might. Hear my prayer, O God; listen to the words of my mouth.
67:4 May the nations be glad and sing for joy, for You (God) rule the peoples justly and guide the nations of the earth.
89:14 Righteousness and justice are the foundation of Your throne; love and faithfulness go before You.
94:2 Rise up, O Judge of the earth; pay back to the proud what they deserve.
101:1 I will sing of Your love and justice; to You, O Lord, I will sing praise.
103:6 The Lord works righteousness and justice for all the oppressed.

God is righteous

36:5-6 Your love, O Lord, reaches to the heavens, Your faithfulness to the skies. Your righteousness is like the mighty mountains, Your justice like the great deep.
51:10-12 Create in me a pure heart, O God, and renew a steadfast spirit within me. Do not cast me from Your presence or take Your Holy Spirit from me. Restore to me the joy of Your salvation and grant me a willing spirit, to sustain me.
71:2 Rescue me and deliver me in Your righteousness; turn Your ear to me and save me.
71:15 My mouth will tell of Your righteousness, of Your salvation all day long, though I know not its measure.
71:16 I will proclaim Your might acts, O Sovereign Lord; I will proclaim Your righteousness, Yours alone.

71:19 Your righteousness reaches to the skies, O God, You who have done great things. Who, O God, is like You?

71:23-24 My lips will shout for joy when I sing praise to You-I, whom You have redeemed. My tongue will tell of Your righteous acts all day long

85:13 Righteousness goes before Him (God) and prepares the way for His steps.

89:14 Righteousness and justice are the foundation of Your throne; love and faithfulness go before You.

89:15-16 Blessed are those who have learned to acclaim You, who walk in the light of Your presence, O Lord. They rejoice in Your name all day long; they exalt in Your righteousness.

103:6 The Lord works righteousness and justice for all the oppressed.

111:3 Glorious and majestic are His deeds, and His righteousness endures forever.

116:5 The Lord is gracious and righteous; our God is full of compassion.

119:123 My eyes fail, looking for Your salvation, looking for Your righteous promise.

143:1 O Lord, hear my prayer, listen to my cry for mercy; in Your faithfulness and righteousness come to my relief.

143:11 For Your name's sake, O Lord, preserve my life; in Your righteousness, bring me out of trouble.

145:7 People will celebrate Your abundant goodness and joyfully sing of Your righteousness.

145:17 The Lord is righteous in all His ways and loving toward all He has made.

About the Author

Robert M. Gullberg, M.D. is from Park Ridge, Illinois and has practiced Internal Medicine for over 30 years. His father was a dentist and practiced for over 40 years, many of those years as a volunteer at the Pacific Garden Mission in Chicago, Illinois. Both of his parents, and siblings Jim, Lin and Laurie have been believers and encouraged him in the Christian faith.

He attended Northwestern University in Evanston, Illinois and then graduated from the University of Illinois Medical School . As a senior in medical school, he got a glimpse of global missions when he worked in a missionary hospital in Herbertpur, India near the Nepalian border for 3 months. From the University of Illinois, he headed to Evanston Hospital and completed a residency in Internal Medicine. Next was a two-year Fellowship in the study of Infections at NU Medical School in Chicago. He moved to Racine, Wisconsin in 1986 and has practiced medicine there for over three decades.

His journey with the Lord began at age 13 at the Northwest Covenant Church in Mt. Prospect, Illinois. Since then, Dr. Bob has led Bible studies for 40 years on many topics from Genesis to Revelation at an evangelical church in Racine, Wisconsin.

He has been a practicing internist for years and has kept busy taking care of a load of thousands of patients. There are occasions every day to see God work his miracles in his patients. One of his goals in life is to get know the Bible as well as he knows medicine. He hopes your goal is similar; to know the heartbeat of God through the Scriptures. Knowing Psalms will help you to GO TO GOD FIRST with all your everyday problems.

He lives in Wisconsin with his wife Janet and has four adult children.

Table of Contents- Part Two
Psalms for Wellness

'Psalms for Wellness' is Part Two of the book and will help you get closer to God by meditating on Psalms. It is divided into **two sections**: *Learning to Go to God First* in the many circumstances of your life and *Knowing God Better through the Psalms*. They will enhance your individual or corporate prayer life.

Table of Contents

PART TWO

King David knew God *extremely* well. He ascribed to God over **100 attributes** in Psalms. Why don't you learn from David? God will reveal insights into His character from Psalms that will give you a glimpse of His glory. Part Two is a useful resource for individual or corporate prayer.

Made in the USA
Monee, IL
09 February 2021